HOW TO

PROFIT FROM
PET PRODUCTS

HOW TO

PROFIT FROM PET PRODUCTS

ALISON JONES

ELMSBURY

First published in Great Britain in 2012 by Elmsbury Publishing UK

Copyright © 2012 Elmsbury Publishing UK
Text copyright © 2012 Alison Jones

10 9 8 7 6 5 4 3 2 1

A CIP catalogue record for this book is available from the British Library.

ISBN 978-0-9574878-0-2

Typeset in Liberation
Printed and bound in Great Britain

www.elmsbury.com

Contents

Preface

I can still remember the moment that I discovered the profit potential of pet accessories, back in May 2006. Having bought ten £1 'blingy' dog collars from a beach shop whilst on holiday, I got home, listed them on eBay, and watched each of them receive bids of £10-14 each. Just a few months later, after hours of market and supplier research, I was opening my first bulk consignment of pet collars. Prince & Princess Petwear was born.

Back then, the designer pet accessories industry was still very much in its infancy, and there was little information (and certainly no books!) available on retailing designer pet accessories. Luckily, I was reading for a Business and Management Degree at the time, and therefore fortunate enough to know a team of business lecturers, all experts in their specialist subjects, whom I could approach whenever I encountered a problem or needed advice. I had also managed to gain a rather well-connected start-up adviser from St Helens Chamber of Commerce for the first two years of the business' life.

Unfortunately, most business owners don't have the luxury of having their own 'team of experts' to provide business advice, support, and motivation. I hope, however, that *How to Profit from Pet Products* will go a small way to impart the advice and knowledge that I have been given and have learned along the way. I hope too, that this book will inspire both seasoned pet accessories retailers, and those who are *just thinking about it*, and help them on their way to building a successful and profitable business.

Ali Jones,
Founder, Prince & Princess Petwear

Acknowledgements

First and foremost, I would like to thank Elsmbury, and my editor Kath Schonewille for her invaluable guidance and hard work. Any remaining errors are entirely my own.

It is my customers who inspired me to write this book, and I particularly wish to thank those that have taken the time to share their experiences, triumphs, and failures, with me over the years.

Thanks to all of my lecturers at St Helens College School of Business and Management 2004-09, and my adviser at St Helens Chamber during the first few years of trading. Without their knowledge and advice, Prince and Princess Petwear, and this book, would not have been possible.

I'd like to give a special thanks to my parents for their encouragement and for teaching me that determination and perseverance always pays off. Thanks also to my sister, who gave up part of her kitchen table so that I had somewhere quiet to write this book, and all of its re-drafts!

Last but not least, to The Bobs for their unwavering support, and to the critics who don't maintain radio silence.

The Routes to a Pet Products Business

There are many different ways to enter the designer pet accessories market. You may be thinking about becoming (or already be) a specialist pet products business, perhaps with a pet accessories website or pet shop.

Existing businesses that already operate in the pet industry, such as dog groomers, may diversify into retail to generate an extra income and increase their customer base. Selling pet accessories isn't just confined to businesses already operating within the pet industry though. There are an increasing number of gift shops, clothing boutiques, and garden centres, among others, which are enjoying the gains of expansion into products for the four-legged friends of their customers.

Whichever route you take, there are a number of factors that you will need to consider, which will help to improve your chances of success.

The Specialist Pet Accessories Business

The specialist focuses only on offering pet accessories, which means that they can concentrate on retail without having to juggle an additional activity such as dog grooming or breeding. To succeed, the specialist should consider the following:

Provide Something Different

There are countless companies out there that focus on offering just pet accessories. It is tempting for business owners to study these competitors with the aim of imitating them, especially if you are starting up with no previous experience of retail or the pet industry. Instead of mimicking and becoming a clone, (and copying a rival's mistakes in the process), specialists should look for ways to distinguish their business from the competition. There are many ways to do this, including by offering a unique range of products, or a personal shopping service.

You could also differentiate your business by offering a service, such as grooming or pet whispering. Even if you don't have the necessary skills you can always rent out a room to another specialist.

Become Even More Special

In a market with a high level of competition, it helps if you can find a corner of the market that is not currently being served by another company, is growing, and whose target customers have specific problems that you can solve. Some specialist shops are so niche they have become world-renowned simply because they are the only outlet selling a particular product or range. Even though these businesses serve a smaller number of customers than they would if they catered for everyone, they can charge a premium for their specialist products.

To find your niche, you will need to think of a specific group of customers you can serve, such as the owners of a particular breed (e.g., Peterbald cats), or size of animal (e.g., giant rabbits), or owners that take part in specific activities (e.g., CaniX). It always helps if you have a passion for your chosen niche area.

Become an Expert

Customers expect pet product retailers to be knowledgeable in a wide range of issues relating to their pets. They will ask what size coat will fit their dog, what shampoo they should buy for their coarse-haired pet, which toys they should buy to stop their cat clawing their furniture, etc.

Obviously, if you have a niche and focus on a particular animal or breed, or if your business is built around a single innovative product, then you won't need to have such an extensive knowledge, but you will still need to know your products, and the animals that they are intended for, in-depth.

The Diversified Business

E xisting businesses that start selling pet accessories can generate an extra income without having to find extra customers through expensive marketing. There are two types of diversification: lateral (pet related), and horizontal (non-pet related).

Pet-Related Diversification

Selling pet accessories can provide an extra income, and attract new customers to businesses that already offer a pet-related service such as:

- Grooming salons and mobile
- Boarding kennels, catteries, & pet hotels
- Day care
- Dog trainers, dog walkers, and pet-sitters
- Veterinary practices
- Dog hydrotherapy
- Breeding
- Pet photographers
- Pet charities

To succeed the pet-related diversifier should consider the following:

Capitalise on Trust

Professional businesses, such as grooming salons, dog trainers, veterinary practices, and hydrotherapy providers, are entrusted with the care, health, and well-being of pets.

This presents a good opportunity to make additional income by capitalising on the confidence that customers already have in them. This is by no means taking advantage; you will need to offer products that match the quality of the services that you already provide.

The Guilt Factor

Many owners feel guilty for leaving their pets at boarding kennels, catteries, day care, or taking their pet for an appointment at a veterinary clinic. The more guilt that owners feel, the more money they are likely to spend on gifts and luxuries, such as toys, treats, and pampering packs.

Provide Above the Expected

In certain pet-related service businesses, customers expect to see at least a small selection of pet products. Take for example veterinary surgeries, which are probably not the first place that comes to mind as a place to buy pet accessories. However, waiting rooms with a display of pet products beyond the special dietary food and Elizabethan collars can be a nice distraction and generate a healthy extra income.

Provide Convenience

Selling pet accessories alongside a service such as dog grooming, provides convenience for customers as they can see, touch, and feel the products, and try them on their pets when they visit.

'Mobile' businesses, such as pet sitters, mobile groomers, and dog walkers and trainers, can provide even more convenience. Many clients who use these services are busy people, and therefore, you can save them a trip to an out of town pet store or having to shop online, by bringing your selection of products directly to their home.

Impulse Buying

At the point of sale it can be much easier to get customers to add products to their bill. They are, after all, about to make payment for your pet services, so in their minds, a few extra pounds on top of a service or consultation fee won't make much difference.

Low value impulse items placed strategically at a till point can increase the 'basket value' of each sale.

Use Products to Sell Them

If you can incorporate the products that you sell into the delivery of your service, you may be able to promote more sales. Dog trainers, for example, may find that they can sell to their clients the same clickers, toys, and treats that they use as part of their training exercises. A dog hotel could sell the same handmade beds and designer feeding bowls that feature in its rooms.

However, some businesses need to be careful that they don't

lower the demand for their service by offering products that are an integral part of their core business. Selling shampoos and finishing sprays in a grooming salon, for instance, may result in clients visiting less often. On the other hand, by selling in small sizes, your clients will run out more frequently and will have to return to you to purchase more, and this may increase your bookings.

Improve your Resource Efficiency

By diversifying, you can make better use of your existing resources and improve your efficiency. Perhaps there is an unused space in your premises that could be filled with a range of pet products. If you are a trainer, pet sitter, or walker that visits clients regularly, perhaps you could make better use of each visit by providing a mail order service.

If you own a website that merely details the service you offer, you might feel that you could take advantage of the traffic visiting your site by transforming it into an ecommerce shop and generating revenue from it directly.

Non-Pet Related Diversification

I t may come as a surprise to some, but you can sell pet accessories in a wide variety of businesses, not just the obvious outlets such as pet shops. This is good news if you are already running a business that seemingly has no association with the pet industry, including:

- Fashion boutiques
- Garden centres and DIY shops
- Farm shops
- Department stores
- Gift shops
- Equestrian businesses

- Craftspeople

To diversify successfully, these businesses should consider the following:

Specialists Think 'Equivalents'

Offering a complete range of pet products is unlikely to be practical for all but the largest of non-pet related businesses. However, if pets are important to your customers, you should try to find a way to develop your specialist range to include products for pets, whilst remaining loyal to the area of expertise for which you are renowned. A biscuit manufacturer could turn their hand to producing dog treats, for example. A jewellery boutique could offer pet necklaces, tags and collars incorporating precious jewels (think Hartman & Rose,) a furniture store could sell furniture for pets, a leather goods business could sell leather dog carriers and collars, a ceramics maker could create unique pet feeding bowls, a fashion store could sell pet clothing ... Basically, if there is a corresponding product for pets, then you may be able to generate a good extra income from it.

Provide the Unexpected and the Expected

Selling pet accessories in unexpected places can provide a talking point for customers and the Press, which can increase the success of diversification, as well as help your business stand out from the rest. A good example of this is US retailer Icing by Claire's, which sells pet clothing in its stores alongside its jewellery and fashion accessories.

Sometimes the unexpected can become the norm when a market leader diversifies into pet products and then everyone else copies. It is now commonplace to see pet products in garden centres, and there is a growing trend for department stores to include a pet section, (this is no doubt thanks to the success of The Pet Department in Harrods, London.) However, the absence of pet products in certain business types can be a red flag to a customer.

Seasonality

Selling pet accessories can help businesses to overcome any seasonal lows. Garden centres, for instance, traditionally struggled to get people through their doors during the winter months, but many have responded by opening cafes, gift and home ware departments, apparel boutiques and ... pet shops Diversifying into pet products can help bring in a steady stream of revenue throughout the year.

Beware of the Risks

Diversifying into an area in which you have no prior experience can be risky. After all, you are putting your reputation, which you have built on some other product or service, on the line. You will want to attract new customers without putting off your existing ones, so the decision to start retailing pet products must be accepted by your target market.

Entering a new market is likely to take up more of your time and may require you to learn new skills and knowledge. It can be difficult to give sufficient time to a new venture if your primary business is demanding constant attention. The danger is that the challenge of diversifying may hamper your overall effectiveness and productivity, and this may damage the reputation of both your new and old business.

However, the decision to diversify is sometimes one that is made when a business has reached a plateau in terms of revenue, and it needs to find new customers and markets to survive. In these cases, there is little or nothing to lose.

In the next chapter, we will look at how to gather research on your target market, including the questions you will need to ask potential customers, in order to gain valuable information that you can use in every aspect of your pet business.

Understanding the Market

B efore launching a new business or diversifying into pet accessories, you will need to research the market.

Factors, such as customers, competitors, and the external environment, can affect businesses in different ways, so it is vital that you do thorough research before you launch, and at regular intervals thereafter.

Some business owners believe that research is not necessary. They make the mistake of thinking that by imitating a successful competitor, or by making assumptions such as "If I like vibrant-coloured pet toys then my customers will too," they can build a thriving business. Others cite a lack of time as a reason for not doing enough research, so later in this chapter we shall look at the ways to save time by incorporating market research into other business activities.

Two Types of Data

There are two types of data that you will need to collect: primary, and secondary.

Primary Data

Primary data is information that you gather yourself firsthand from a group of people that are representative of your target market. Probably the most popular primary data method used is the questionnaire because you can obtain data from a large sample of people quite cheaply, and it is relatively easy to analyse the data afterwards.

Interviews are another popular method, as you can gain a lot of in-depth information from individuals either over the phone or face to face. However, due to the time it takes to recruit and interview enough people, this method is usually only used when there is a lot of money at stake, such as when researching and developing a new product.

A focus group is a small number of people that meet to discuss a topic in-depth, such as the problems they encounter as pet owners. It usually takes a lot of preparation and a highly skilled researcher to steer a focus group without influencing the research. However, an informal brainstorming session with friends or customers may be just as productive, and certainly cheaper to implement, providing the members of the group can contribute constructively.

Mystery shopping is a legitimate method of gathering data on a competitor. By posing as a genuine customer, you can to find out a lot about the competition including how they treat customers, the prices they charge, the level of competence of staff, and the overall shopping experience they provide. In some cases, visiting a shop or telephoning may be the only way to find out information about them.

Secondary Data

Secondary data is information that has been produced or collected by someone else. Secondary sources include:

- Magazine and newspaper articles
- Websites, blogs, and pet forums
- Government statistics
- Research reports
- Company documents
- Brochures, flyers, and leaflets
- Factual TV programmes e.g., news, documentaries
- Chamber of Commerce or business advisory service
- Social and business network sites
- Customer reviews

Collecting Your Data

C ounter-intuitively, it is best to collect secondary data first as it could give you an indication about the areas you need to focus on for your primary research, as well as the best methods to collect it.

There are three main areas of research you should cover; your potential customers; your competitors; and external factors such as the economy and legislation.

Your Potential Customers

The aim of analysing your prospective customers is to identify the markets you should be targeting, and to find out their needs and wants so that your company can fulfil them.

Basic Information – What is their age, gender, job, income, location, marital status, lifestyle, children, and hobbies?

Pet Ownership – What types, breeds, ages, and number of pets are in their household? What is the reason for ownership (family pet, companion, breeding, showing)?

Shopping Habits – Where do they buy pet accessories (online, pet shop, etc)? Which shops do they currently buy from? How much and how often do they spend on their pets? How much and how often do they purchase various pet products? What features do they look for (colour, durability, familiar brand name, designer style)? Are they spending more, the same, or less on their pets than they were a year ago? What is their minimum and maximum spend for various pet products? How far are they are willing to travel to buy pet accessories?

Attitudes and Opinions – What do people think about aspects of your existing or proposed business (such as your pricing, branding, and product range)? What are their attitudes towards existing products on the market? What are their favourite and their least favourite pet brands, and why? Which, if any, social networking sites do they use?

Issues and Challenges – What problems have they encountered in the course of owning or shopping for their pets and how could your business solve these problems? Have they bought products from abroad because they are unavailable in the UK? What good or bad experiences have they had whilst shopping for pet products? What ideas do they have for your products, services, pricing, etc?

Your Competitors

The aim of analysing your competitors is to discover their strengths and weaknesses, what makes them successful, and ultimately identify gaps in the market.

Identify competitors – How many players are in the market? How many businesses will be in direct competition with you (because they have the same business as you), and who will be in indirect competition with you (because they run a similar business)? How much do they dominate? Are there any opportunities to take some of their market share?

History & Operations – How long they have been trading? How many staff do they employ? What are their hours of operation? Have they recently moved into bigger premises or diversified into new markets, or do they appear to be downsizing? What is the size of their operation (do they have a warehouse or are they a home-based business)? What are their policies (do they offer free delivery, extended returns)? What price strategies and sales channels do they use? What are their future plans?

Products – How extensive is their product range? Will they be directly competing with you? Do their products and services address specific problems their customers have? Are their products innovative? Which brands do they stock? Do they have any exclusive licensing agreements? What products and services do they provide that you don't or can't?

Revenue - A competitor's revenue is often difficult to find out. However, for a nominal fee you can download the accounts and other documents of limited companies from CompaniesHouse.gov.uk. Occasionally though, you'll encounter a business that is happy to report what their turnover is, as the owners of Dog Bling did when they appeared on BBC's Dragons Den.

Marketing – What media do your competitors use to promote themselves (website, magazine adverts, social media)? How regularly do they advertise? Are they using Pay Per Click advertising? Which groups of people do they appear to be targeting? Do they capture customer details by offering a newsletter or other incentive? What is their marketing budget? Do they use any social networking sites?

Service - How well do they build relationships with customers over the phone, by email, or in person? Do they ask customers the right questions? How do they encourage people to buy? Are they knowledgeable about the products that they are selling? What after-sales care do they offer? Do they offer loyalty schemes or other incentives?

Customers – What do customers love and dislike about your competitors? Why do they keep buying from them or why did they stop? What have people written about the service, products, and other aspects of their business on review sites and blogs?

The External Environment

The aim of examining the external environment is to identify possible factors that could impact how your business operates, its costs, and consumer demand.

Economic – How does an economic downturn affect the buying behaviour of pet owners (do they reduce their spending on pet products by buying products with a lower ticket price or by buying less frequently?) How do improvements in the economy affect buying behaviour (do more people get pets, does spending increase?) How will exchange rates, taxation, interest rates, and import legislation have an impact on your business?

Social – How are the demographic factors of the population changing? Are households with pets increasing? What current buying trends exist amongst pet owners? What attitudes exist towards buying healthy, eco-friendly, organic, handmade, British-made, and foreign-made pet products? How do topical news debates such as 'should pets wear clothes' affect buyer behaviour? How do celebrities influence buyer behaviour? Which social networking sites are most popular? Could your business capitalise on big events such as The World Cup?

Technological – What advances in technology could affect how you communicate with, and market to, your customers in the future? How often will your website become outdated (due to new design trends, changes in payment technology, screen-resolution updates, etc?) Will the increase in mobile phone usage change how your customers buy from you in the future? Will you be able to afford to keep up to date with technological advances? Will you still be able to compete if you cannot afford to adopt new technologies?

Political – How will changes in taxation, trading and employment laws affect your business? How could possible future government legislation, such as all dogs having to be microchipped, have an impact? Are their any government grants available to your business? Are there any buy local initiatives in your area and what impact will they have on your business? What new laws and directives are due to come into force in the future and how could they affect your business?

Environmental – How will the growing concerns about the environment affect you? What new markets have been created due to the raised awareness of climate change? How will the weather affect your sales, product ranges, and insurance premiums?

Legal – How will the Sale of Goods Act (1979) affect how you operate and source products? How will advertising laws affect your marketing? Will employment laws such as the Working Time Directive and the Health and Safety at Work Act (1974) increase your costs? How will the Distance Selling Regulations (2000) affect your terms and conditions? What other laws are relevant to your business?

Analysing & Making Conclusions

O nce you have collected your data, you will need to analyse your findings. Presenting the data in pie charts and graphs will make it easy to identify any patterns and form conclusions. Not all data will lend itself to being shown in a chart though, (if, for instance, the responses to some open questions are long or are diverse.)

Drawing conclusions will help you decide how best to proceed with each of the elements that make up your business (branding, pricing, product range, etc) and ultimately whether it will be a viable enterprise.

Figure 2.1 gives examples of some possible conclusions you could make about your findings. Most conclusions are common sense, but some are not always obvious and may require further investigation. For example, it would be simple to identify a large number of dog owners in your sample and conclude that you need to focus on selling dog products, but what conclusion would you make about someone who travels ten miles to a pet boutique, when there is a pet shop two streets away? Perhaps the boutique's opening times are more convenient, it is the nearest stockist of a popular brand, or maybe the customer is simply not aware that the local shop exists. Sometimes there are many possible explanations for one finding, so obtaining permission to contact your sample again, to get further clarification if you need it, can help you avoid jumping to the wrong conclusions.

Figure 2.1 Examples of Findings and Possible Conclusions

Finding	Possible Conclusion
Some of your sample like taking their dogs for country walks.	Customers may need waterproof jackets, protective car blankets, hi-vis products, deep cleansing grooming products.
Your sample buys pet accessories that are durable, reliable, and safe.	Your branding, products, and core values needs to reflect these values in order to appeal to them.
There are several pet shops in town, but none are customer-orientated.	Competition is high, so you will need to be sure you can offer a better service and that customers will be willing to try a new pet shop. If not, find another location.
Some of your sample takes their pets to shows.	Customers will need professional grooming products, carriers, and products for travel sickness and anxiety.
The government is planning to increase the minimum wage.	You may need to sell more products or increase prices to break even, or cut costs (e.g., reduce staff hours.)
The majority of your sample owns just one type of animal or breed.	You should focus on offering products for that animal or breed, as long as you think that the niche will be lucrative.
The sample buys both high- and low-end products.	You may need to offer a range of products with different price points.
A local campaign to get more people buying fair trade and eco-friendly products is due to launch.	If you think the campaign will strike a chord with consumers you should stock fair trade products or publicise how eco-friendly your business is.

Ongoing Market Research

P eople tend to be better at conducting market research before launching a business or diversifying into a new market. Once launched, owners are often far too busy with the day-to-day running of the business to find time to update their research. Furthermore, some owners fail to realise just how rapidly trends, customers, competitors, and other external factors can change.

Fortunately, ongoing market research doesn't have to be a massive drain on your time and resources, as it is something that can be easily incorporated into other business activities to help you stay one step ahead and meet changing customer needs.

Monitoring Customers

You can conduct market research every time you engage with your customers. The odd question dropped into a friendly conversation, a suggestion box, or a brief online questionnaire, will not only garner valuable information, but also show your customers that you are interested in their opinions, which will help you to build rapport.

If you plan to use social networking sites, such as Twitter and Facebook, to promote your business, you can use them to pose research questions and get people to vote for possible new products for your range, too.

Instead of just giving away discounts and other incentives, you can make customers earn some of their rewards by getting them to take part in market research. A quick questionnaire in exchange for 5% off, for instance, will benefit both you and the customer. You could even consider establishing a VIP group of select customers willing to test products and complete surveys regularly in exchange for exclusive offers.

If you collect the same data continuously (such as customer

satisfaction surveys,) you should try to automate this where possible to save yourself time. For example, online shops must send out a confirmation email when a customer places an order. You can use this opportunity to include a link inviting recipients to answer an e-survey, which you can set up using an online survey software company such as SurveyMonkey.com. You can then regularly monitor the findings to check if you are improving.

Monitoring Competitors

Monitoring your competitors will be less time-consuming if you can create a matrix such as in the example in Figure 2.2.

Figure 2.2 Example of a Competitor Analysis Matrix

	Competitor A	Competitor B
Products	Sells cat and small animal products	Dogs-only products
Channels	Online	Shop, Online, & Events
Strengths	Offers customers a choice of delivery options, free returns, and a guarantee. Website is professional and on-trend.	Has been trading for fifteen years. Launches new promotions regularly. Has brand exclusivity.
Weaknesses	Doesn't have a big product range (although this is growing.)	Not well known outside of the town, has dated website, and poor customer policies.
Action	Increase product range, review delivery options and customer policies.	Try to gain exclusivity of a brand, and launch more promotions.

With a matrix, you can monitor as many aspects of your rival's business that you feel are important such as their pricing policies, service, corporate identity, marketing, and promotions.

A final column, 'Action', can be used to identify the gaps your competitors have left and the course of action, if any, you need to take to improve your competitive position.

You may have a list of twenty or thirty competitors depending on your business' situation, but you only need to examine a few of these each week to stay up-to-date. As you will only be looking for *changes* that your competitors have made rather than collecting the information from scratch, you will need only to set aside a short amount of time to monitor them.

Online retailers are easy to monitor, but if some of your rivals are bricks and mortar businesses, you can check up on them whilst doing your own shopping to save time. If you ever stand at pet exhibitions, use your breaks to check out the competition.

Monitoring the External Environment

It is always wise when running a business to pay attention to any local, national, and international news stories on external factors (see page 25.) A quick scan of the news pages on the internet, or a listen to the business news on the radio on the way to work, can alert you to any forthcoming issues and give you time to plan ahead. Trade publications such as Pet Product Marketing often cover national and general business news stories, but discuss the affect that the issues have specifically on the pet industry, which should make monitoring external factors more straightforward.

Networking not only helps you raise awareness of your business, but you can learn a lot about what is happening in your locality, giving you more time to react, which can potentially provide you with an edge over competitors.

In the next chapter, we will look at the sales channels you can use to reach your target market, together with their set up and running costs, customer expectations, and profitability.

Choosing the Right Sales Channels

C hoosing the right sales outlets is about deciding the best way to deliver information and products to your target market. Thanks to the advent of the internet, and most recently the smart phone, businesses now have more sales channels to choose from than ever before:

- Retail premises
- Online
- Mobile commerce
- E-marketplaces
- Mail order
- Telemarketing
- Events
- Direct sales

The sales channels you choose are an integral factor in your ability to make a profit.

Multi-Channel Retailing

M ulti-channel retailing, or selling through more than one channel, is an effective strategy for many pet retailers and a proven way to develop the customer shopping experience and increase revenue and growth.

You are likely to reach and capture a broader range of customers if you are operating more than one channel, not least because prospective customers tend to be reassured by a business that has expanded into two or more channels.

Multi-channel retailing can improve the efficiency of an operation through better sharing of its resources. For example, if you buy a van to run direct sales, you could also use that van to attend pet shows, and thus use it to generate more revenue. Moreover, you can benefit from economies of scale, whereby the more sales you generate across the channels the cheaper it becomes because you'll be using your equipment and time more efficiently.

Another benefit, which can become apparent if one sales channel starts under-performing, is that you have the other channels to fall back on. This may also mean that you have an advantage over rivals who rely on just one channel, particularly if a problem is industry- or retail-wide.

Having more than one channel enables you to set different prices for your products based on each channel's target audience, location, and overheads. This strategy can cause a few headaches though if a customer discovers that a product they bought on your website would have been cheaper in your shop, for example.

Customers increasingly expect to have an integrated shopping and brand experience. For example, if a customer buys an item on your website, they expect to be able to return it to your store. Similarly, they like to know that if they spot a pet bed on your stall, they can order it later from your web or mobile-optimised site once they've checked the measurements.

Stock keeping, bookkeeping, and other administrative tasks could become more time-consuming and trickier to manage, and ideally you should integrate these systems into a single system that all of your channels can share. Multi-channel systems, whether they are off the shelf or bespoke, can be expensive, but they will help you achieve consistency across your brand.

Choosing The Right Channels

Whether you choose to sell pet products through one channel, or several, you need to ensure that the channel(s) you choose will:

- **Reach your target market** – Will you be able to reach enough potential customers through the new channel? Which channels do your existing and potential customers prefer?

- **Be cost effective** – A pet shop that decides to start selling online for example, needs to take into account the initial out-lay of designing and launching a site, as well as the ongoing costs such as search engine optimisation, and site maintenance. It may take time and a lot of hard work before you break-even, so you need to be certain that a new channel can generate enough extra income to make it worthwhile

- **Offer customers integrated brand experience** – Can customers that bought a product from your website then return it to your shop if they need to? Are you able to offer the same or a larger product range across your channels? Offering an integrated brand experience can be an issue for small businesses as it means all your systems, such as EPoS (Electronic Point of Sale), need to be built-in together to work centrally.

- **Match your business values and vision** – If your business is all about being eco-friendly, then launching a gas-guzzling sales van is hardly supporting that vision. If your business is keen to provide a personal service, you are more likely to achieve this with premises, events, or direct selling, rather than a website.

Over the following subchapters, we'll look in-depth at the most appropriate channels for selling pet accessories, what customers expect, the level of competition you'll face, and if they will generate a good profit.

Sales Channels: Premises

Having a shop can be a highly rewarding and lucrative way to sell pet accessories. It can be a lot of hard work, and involve long hours, but it offers social interaction with customers, and an opportunity to become an integral part of a community.

Understandably, the almost daily reports about the disappearing high street discourage people from opening new shops. For every closure though, there are many more stories of businesses having success, even those in the shadow of large competitors such as Pets at Home.

A major plus to running a shop, is that customers tend to perceive a business with physical premises as being more trustworthy.

Customer Expectations

When shopping in a small independent store, customers expect a personal experience provided by friendly staff. They like to be acknowledged when they enter and invited to approach staff for help if they need it. Staff should be knowledgeable in every product's benefits and features and be able to recommend products to solve pet related issues.

The interior of your shop needs to be inviting, clean, and un-cluttered. People expect to be able to find what they are looking for quickly and easily, so a good layout, clear signage, and accessible shelving are essential. A good range is favourable, as is having transparent pricing on all of your products because many customers won't ask the price of items.

A delivery service or 'order online and collect in store' facility is something to consider too.

Finally, your shop should be more than just a shop. Increasingly, there is a demand for retailers to create 'social hubs', by arranging events and activities for customers.

Costs

There are arguably greater overheads associated with having premises than any other sales channel. These include:

Premises
Finding the right premises can be a long process, and usually ends in a trade-off between rent (or mortgage) and factors such as location, accessibility and floor space. If you plan to rent premises, then you'll need to put down a deposit (typically up to six months' rent in advance.) Furthermore, landlords will try to tie you in to lengthy lease agreements.

Business Rates and Stamp Duty

Business rates are a tax imposed by local authorities on the occupiers of commercial property, and is based on a valuation of the premises. Sometimes these may be included in the rent. You will need to pay stamp duty, which is payable on all commercial leases.

Utilities, Maintenance, and Repair

An ongoing cost associated with having a shop is utilities. If you own a business property rather than rent, then you are also responsible for maintenance, repairs, building and contents insurance, and anything else that a landlord would normally take care of.

Fixtures, Fittings, and Signage

To keep customers in your shop for as long as possible, the interior must be appealing and inviting. You will need to have good display fittings. These can be expensive, so check with suppliers to find out if they can supply Point of Sale units with their products, as this could reduce your costs quite considerably. Good lighting is essential, not only for safety, but to show products off to their best. Professional signage is an important part of your branding, and, if you have a large shop floor, interior signs can help customers to find what they are looking for.

Stock

The amount of stock you need will depend on the floor space of your shop and the type of display units you have. Obviously, the more stock you buy the longer it will take to break even. To reduce your stock expenditure you could try to negotiate with a supplier who will offer goods on a sale or return basis.

Legal

If you have customers visiting your premises then public liability insurance is a legal requirement. Product liability is also worth considering if it is not included. Insurance companies do not usually consider selling pet accessories to be high risk, so premiums are unlikely to be excessive unless you are also offering a service such as veterinary care.

Advertising

If you are a newly launched business you will probably need to spend quite a bit on advertising initially to get customers through your doors. Existing businesses diversifying into retail can usually take advantage of the mailing list they've built up and promote directly to customers to keep costs down.

Competition

Competitor research is vital because it will help you find the right location for your shop and identify whether a competitor really is a competitor. (Sometimes customers buy from shops out of necessity rather than loyalty, and, given a choice, would quite happily switch allegiance.)

The competition from larger pet store chains, supermarkets, and the huge number of online businesses can cause the independent shop owner many a sleepless night. However, if you can focus on the things that your larger competitors find difficult to do, such as offering a personal shopping experience, bringing out new products quickly, and excellent customer service, then you will be well on your way to gaining a competitive edge.

Profitability

To be profitable, the location of your premises is important. Your shop obviously needs to be wherever your target market is, but other factors such as passing trade, customer parking, public transport links, and the reputation of the area, need to be sufficient before you can earn back your initial outlay and continual costs, and generate a profit.

Having retail premises is one of the most expensive channels for a business, so keeping tight control of your outgoings is vital. It helps if you offer a service alongside retailing pet products, to achieve better cost and resource efficiency.

People trust a shop more than any other channel because it is seemingly more permanent and stable, and it allows them to interact with staff. In addition, studies have shown that customers are more likely to buy a product when they go to a shop because they can touch and feel the products.

Sales Channels: Online

Without a doubt, the internet has transformed the way we buy and sell. No longer are business owners required to man the till to make sales. With ecommerce, your website is a shop that has neither geographical boundaries nor closing times.

The adoption of internet shopping has made it easier for existing businesses to expand and reach a global audience, whilst taking advantage of few extra overheads. Even stay-at-home mums and those with full-time jobs have been able to benefit by launching their own online pet business from their spare room. However, this increased accessibility has resulted in fierce competition in the pet industry.

Companies entering this sales channel must be able to keep pace with the ever-changing technology and needs of its customers. There are however, a number of low cost, and even free ways, to achieve this.

Customer Expectations

Customers expect a smooth and secure shopping process with clear pricing and delivery charges. They also expect to be given an estimated delivery time, and to receive their goods swiftly, often within a day of placing an order. Offering favourable policies, such as free returns, helps to reassure customers, and it reduces any pre-purchase anxiety they may have when ordering online.

People who shop for pet products online want to be able to find what they are looking for quickly and easily, so a good search function is essential. Customers aren't merely looking for pet products though; they are seeking information and advice to assist them in the buying process and pet ownership. A credible online shop that knows everything there is to know about pets and pet accessories is bound to be a hit with buyers.

For customers, the major downside of shopping online is not being able to touch and feel products before they buy. High quality images that can zoom-in, customer photos, and videos demonstrations can all help reduce the uncertainty that customers feel and promote more sales.

'Live chat' is becoming an essential facility for online stores, as customers want instant answers to their enquiries. Links to social networking sites such as Google+1 and Facebook are also becoming the norm because customers want to ask their friends what they think of a product before they buy.

Costs

There are a number of fixed and ongoing costs associated with this sales channel, so it is important that you investigate all costs before going ahead.

Functionality

Whether you plan to hire a designer, sign up to an ecommerce solution, or build a website yourself, you need to ensure that your website will meet both your requirements and those of your customers. You should begin by creating a list of website functions that you think will be essential, as well as functions that would be beneficial, but are not crucial to your operations or competitiveness.

Shopping functionality - Some shopping functions you might need:

- Multiple currency and language options
- Discounts/ loyalty scheme
- Ability to order personalised products
- Recommendation engine
- Search engine
- Display products with several variants
- Product image zoom
- Customer accounts and order tracking
- Free from adverts and banners
- Live Chat with customer services
- Gift wrapping option

Back-office functionality - The back-office is where the real magic happens for the online shop owner. Undoubtedly, its key function should be to show all the orders along with their status (paid, packed, despatched, or returned, etc.) Sophisticated websites will perform more functions than just this though, helping you save time and provide better customer service, so it's wise to think about the functions you might need, such as:

- Automated emails to confirm order and dispatch

- Integration with software, e.g., epos, accounting, marketing
- Refund payments
- Integration with e-marketplaces or other sales outlet
- Search Engine Optimisation
- Manage your website from your mobile
- Payment gateway integration
- Own domain name
- Stock control
- Generate invoices, delivery notes, etc
- Calculate postage and taxes
- Statistical data on sales, customers, traffic, etc
- Ability to import CSV files from a drop-shipper

Design and Creation

Once armed with a brief, you can start to investigate the options available to you to getting an online shop:

Build a website from scratch - Out of all the ways to get online, building a new website is generally the most expensive option in terms of time and money. It does, however, ensure that your website looks unique, and has all the features that you need.

Sign up to a fully hosted ecommerce platform - There are numerous ecommerce platforms available, which, for a monthly or annual fee, will provide a ready-made solution for retailers looking to sell pet accessories online. Shopping carts such as Shopify, EKM, Lemonstand, and Jimdo, offer various features for different fees.

Download an open source ecommerce platform - Free, open source platforms such as Magento, Zen Cart, OS Commerce, and Presta Shop, require hosting as well as knowledge of a database file manager such as FileZilla. There is usually some HTML and CSS code knowledge needed to customise your website, although there are templates that you can buy or download free to reduce the amount of designing you'll need to do.

Get a free website and add a payment facility - You can sign up for a basic informational website with Wordpress or Blogger and then add PayPal or Google Checkout payment buttons, or Wordpress' own plugin, to transform it into an online shop. By far the best free ecommerce option currently available though is Weebly. It is fully hosted, has customisable templates and you can use your own domain. Moreover, it is integrated with PayPal and Google Checkout buttons.

If you use Facebook, Vendor Shop Social is a free app that allows you to set up a fully functional webshop on your fan page, and is worth considering even if you choose to set up a separate website.

Domain & Hosting

It doesn't cost much to register a domain name (web address) with a provider such as Go Daddy. Your domain name, or web address, should be easy to remember. The best domain names will tell your customers what you do, and even state your location if you have a geographical territory, such as 'bedfordpetboutique.com'.

It is worth getting both the dot co.uk and dot com in case people type the wrong URL, and to prevent someone from buying the domain and then forwarding your traffic to their own site.

If your website is not hosted, then you will also need to pay for hosting for your website's files, which will cost a few pounds a month.

Increasing your Website's Visibility and Traffic

The weeks and months following your website's launch may see your biggest online advertising expenditure as you push to increase traffic and break even. Pay Per Click Advertising is the most popular method. However, once your website starts to show up naturally in the SERPs (Search Engine Results Pages,) you can reduce this advertising budget.

Search engine optimisation is not a one-off process. As trends change, you will need to modify the keywords you are targeting in order to maintain your rankings. If you are not planning to do this yourself, then you will need to hire a firm to do it for you.

Another way to increase online traffic is by placing adverts on other websites. For these, you will either pay a one-off fee, or ideally pay for the results they yield, such as click-throughs or sales.

Payment Acceptance

Payment gateways, such as Sage Pay, and Google Checkout, process your customer's credit or debit card details, take payment, and then transfer the payment into your bank account. For this service, providers may apply a transaction fee, or a percentage fee of each sale, or both. This may be in addition to an annual fee. The lowest fee chargers may not necessarily be suitable for your business so you'll need to do some research to find the best merchant account for you.

Offline payment methods such as cheques, cash on delivery, and direct bank transfers may not be as popular, but they often don't incur fees.

Competition

Competition can be fierce, so online pet accessories shops need to avoid competing on price and instead focus on gaining a competitive advantage in other ways, such as by building a strong brand, sourcing unique and exciting products, offering great customer service, and providing an amazing online shopping experience.

Your website should match, if not exceed, the standard set by your competitors if you are to any have any chance of getting a foothold in the online pet market. An online shop needs to look visually appealing and professional, and be easy to navigate.

Large online retailers will have bigger budgets for website up-grades, advertising, product development, etc, and therefore you will need to find smart ways of competing with them.

Profitability

An online shop is the perfect partner to all the other sales channels if you are planning to have a multi-channel strategy, but it can be a highly profitable channel in its own right, too.

The biggest hurdle to overcome is getting customers to trust your website and your payment security. Appearance is a big factor in this so you may have to invest a lot initially in order to have a website that appears trustworthy. Generally, initial and ongoing costs are small in relation to the potential return you can make from reaching a huge worldwide audience on the web, and compared to some other sales channels.

Offering favourable policies, such as free returns, helps to reassure customers and reduces any anxiety they may feel when purchasing from a particular online business for the first time. However, anything that slows down the checkout process, such as an extensive list of delivery choices, will give customers more time to change their minds and could reduce your revenue.

A recommendation engine will encourage cross-selling if you have a number of different groups of related products. You can relate products by design, style, purpose, size, animal, colour, brand, and benefits, and this can significantly increase online profit.

Sales Channels: Mobile

M-commerce is the newest addition to the range of sales channels, and is currently experiencing astonishing growth. With the number of devices such as smart-phones and iPads rapidly increasing, experts are predicting that mobile shopping will overtake traditional web sales in the future.

A mobile-optimised site is really just a version of your website aimed at device users; the difference being the layout, navigation, and the amount of information presented. The main advantage is that consumers can browse and buy whenever and wherever they want.

For anyone thinking that m-commerce is just a flash in the pan though, big high street names, including Marks and Spencer, John Lewis, and New Look, have already launched their own mobile shopping sites and apps, and some of their sales successes have been well publicised.

Customer Expectations

Expectations are changing as quickly as the technology. However, as most device users currently just information-gather rather than make purchases, your mobile site needs to focus on providing the right amount of product information, FAQs, and contact details. It is important that there is a clear search function and menu, to enable users to navigate around your site easily. Above all, reassurance about security of payment and personal details is vital to capture sales from those that are confident enough about buying via mobile.

Customers will need to be familiar with your business before they buy via mobile, and they will be expecting the same brand experience that they get from your other channels.

A call now button, or Live Chat facility will enable customers to get in touch instantly, which is what this technology is all about.

Costs

Many of the costs associated with e-commerce, such as payment acceptance, advertising, and postage and packaging, are the same for m-commerce.

Design and Creation

Launching a truly unique mobile site that has all the features you need, will probably require the services of a designer. However, it costs less to create an m-commerce site than it does an e-commerce website. You can sign up for an off-the-shelf mobile store from a provider such as MyMcart, which will charge a monthly or annual fee.

As an alternative, you could test the water with a basic, non-commerce mobile site, and use it to direct traffic to your ecommerce site, or give details of how customers can order from you.

Whichever solution you decide upon, your mobile site must have simple navigation and be viewable on the main mobile systems. Apple iOS, for iPhones and iPads, Blackberry, and Android, with the latter expected to overtake Apple iOS as the most popular system in the future.

Because mobile site design and capabilities is in its infancy, the likelihood of needing to update an m-commerce site is high.

Integration

Ideally, your mobile site should be integrated with your existing ecommerce site so that you won't have to spend time managing and updating a separate back office. Thankfully, a growing number of ecommerce platform providers are offering integrated mobile sites alongside their website solutions, which is much more cost effective.

Competition

The vast majority of pet product retailers are yet to take advantage of the growing number of hand-held devices, so a mobile-optimised site would definitely give a business an edge over competitors that are behind the times.

However, your m-site or app will need to be visually appealing and functional if you want to compete with the big players that not only have trusted names, but also the budget to keep up to date with advances in the technology.

Some experts have forecast pure, mobile-only businesses starting up in the future. While this is a long way off, you could suddenly find yourself competing with some new names in the pet products market.

Profitability

Whilst consumer confidence is growing, current sales via mobile-optimised sites are still relatively low compared to ecommerce. If you are looking for an immediate sales boost, then launching a mobile commerce site is probably not the answer, as there is a long way to go before consumers fully embrace mobile shopping. Until that happens, a mobile site can provide kudos, convenience for technophile-customers, and an edge over the competition since very few businesses in the pet industry currently offer m-commerce.

The initial cost is less than that of a traditional e-commerce site, but you'll still need to invest in a conventional website, as customers are more likely to buy from your mobile site if they have bought from you before online. Even if a customer doesn't place an order using a device, your m-site can still have a part to play in the buying process so its contribution to your profit shouldn't be underestimated.

In the long-term, investing in a mobile site now will pay dividends for your business in the future, as you will be able to capture a wider audience.

Sales Channels: e-marketplaces

E-marketplaces can be a profitable stand-alone sales channel for the pet accessories retailer. They can also be a good launch pad for fledgling businesses, a quick and easy way to get rid of old stock, and a great way to test products on a small scale before launching a full-blown pet boutique or website.

For many customers, an e-marketplace is often the first place they visit whenever they need to buy something. Customers use them to compare products, prices, and features, and very often end up completing a purchase without searching elsewhere.

The most popular e-marketplace is the online auction site eBay, but there are other outlets such as Amazon, Ebid, Etsy (for handmade items), notonthehighstreet.com (for largely British made items from small businesses) and even Facebook, which are equally suited to selling pet products.

Customer Expectations

People who shop on sites such as eBay and Amazon, like to find exactly what they want, quickly and easily. Customers value convenience, so offering a fast delivery service, as well as logical navigation round your 'shop' will aid your success. You must ensure that your product listings are complete, with full product details, along with the description tags filled in so that people can narrow their search and find your items with ease.

Customers will verify a seller's performance and will be looking to see good feedback ratings before they make a purchase. Therefore, you'll need to provide excellent customer service, accurate product descriptions, and deliver on time, to encourage future sales.

Customers like to see clear information about the seller's business, and customer-orientated policies will help to reassure them further.

Finally, customers who shop on auction sites like to believe that they are getting a bargain, so try to mention the RRP or original price of your product in the description, as well as how much money they will save by buying from you.

Costs

Registration
The set up costs of this sales channel are minimal as it is free to register for most auction sites.

If you subscribe to upgrades, such as a shop, featured listings, or statistics, these will increase your outgoings each month, but are worth considering if you think they will help you sell more or increase buyer-confidence.

Listing Templates

You may want to use a template for your listings and shop, to stand out from the competition and present your product information in a more appealing way. Ebay charge a little extra for their own listing templates, but you can buy an off-the-shelf template or get one built for you. There are free templates available too, although you may need to change the HTML code if you want the template to match your own branding and to remove any adverts that the provider has built in.

Photographic Equipment

They say that a picture tells a thousand words, and in categories that have hundreds or even thousands of listings (and there aren't many pet product categories that don't), it is vital that your product images are of the highest quality. That means large, bright images that show the product clearly, accurately, and truthfully. To achieve this, you will need a good camera; anything from eight mega pixels upwards should be good enough.

You should try to take images in natural daylight, although you may prefer to invest in a light tent, which is a relatively cheap piece of equipment that will eliminate shadows and provide a standard background for your images.

Post Production

Even with a good camera and lighting conditions, the images you take may still require improvement. Although you should never over-edit an image, a post-production program such as Photoshop or Adobe Paint Shop will allow you to crop, brighten and remove imperfections, and help your images to stand out from your competitors' in the search results.

Listing Fees

Depending on which e-marketplaces you use, you may be charged for listing items or it may be free. All sites charge a sales commission when you sell a product so you will need to calculate this into your price before you create a listing.

Postage and Packaging

A major ongoing cost associated with this channel is postage and packaging. Sellers can sometimes choose whether to offer 'free' P+P and incorporate it into the selling price (and thus avoid the possibility of receiving negative feedback for high postage charges) or to charge it separately. Some e-marketplaces put a cap on how much postage you can charge. You should experiment to find the best solution for your market.

Using a tracked service will protect you if a piece of mail gets lost in the system, or if you get a dishonest buyer.

Competition

Competition in the designer pet accessories departments of e-marketplaces can be fierce and this can drive prices down. Sellers can gain a competitive advantage by offering unique customised and personalised products, by having customer-orientated policies, excellent customer service, and building up positive feedback.

A major factor in your competitiveness in an e-marketplace is knowing when your target market are browsing and ordering, and then running your listings to coincide with these peak times. Good product listing presentation, including high quality photos and template design, can be the deciding factor for customers when they are selecting which seller to buy from.

Profitability

Although you can start selling on e-marketplaces for very little money upfront, listing fees and sales commission can eat into any profit you may make, so it is important to work out a selling price that will deliver a good profit, before you list any products.

Possibly the biggest threat to your profit though, is the increasing number of manufacturers (many of them from the Far East) selling direct to consumers via e-marketplaces. It is impossible to compete on price with these outfits, but if you are able to offer customised, personalised, one-offs, or limited-addition items, you can charge a premium price and generate a profit. Moreover, by being based in the UK, you can offer a much faster delivery service, and most people are willing to pay a higher price in order to receive their items within a more reasonable timeframe.

Never underestimate the marketing value of a listing. Although the aim of a sales channel is to make a profit, it doesn't always follow that it should generate revenue directly. Sellers that are unable to make adequate money through online marketplaces, view their auction listings merely as cheap adverts that send traffic to their online store, (where they offer a larger range and their overheads are much lower.) Some businesses can build large mailing lists through selling loss leaders on e-marketplaces. They then recuperate their losses by promoting other products and services to these customers.

Sales Channels: Mail Order

The mail order catalogue in its traditional form is dying out. This is largely due to our changing social and shopping habits and the rising costs of paper, printing, and postage. Catalogues may still have a place in pet retailing though, albeit in a more modern form.

The Google Catalogs App, that allows users to view all of their favourite catalogues, is testament to the new wave of demand for brochures in electronic format.

There are companies that provide a downloadable or flash 'click and flick' catalogue, in addition to their online shop (the ultimate catalogue, surely?), just to appease the growing number of tablet users, or people that prefer to print it off to read a hard copy.

An in-store catalogue is a convenient way to offer a large product range without having to stock all of the items. It is thus an ideal solution for premises that are short on space, or if offering a complete product range poses a logistical problem (as in the case of exhibitors that can only transport a limited selection of products in a vehicle.)

Customer Expectations

Just as the delivery method for the catalogue has changed, so too have the expectations of those that shop from them. People expect more than just a list of the products available. Look books, which are popular in fashion retailing, advise readers what products work together, and what they need to buy to achieve each look. These 'catalogues' are packaged as magazines, which present the products in an exciting and helpful way, and simultaneously encourages cross-selling. Whatever your approach, your catalogue should be easy to read, with an appealing layout and well-labelled products.

One benefit of a catalogue is that it provides customers with an alternative to your other sales channels, enabling them to view your range in the comfort of their own home or on the move via a device. They expect to be able to see the same products that are in your shop, exhibition stand or website, and perhaps a few more if your alternative sales channel's offering is limited.

Customers like to have the choice of either downloading a catalogue, viewing it online, or reading a hard copy, (although due to concerns about the environment and increasing use of electronic devices, more people are opting for the electronic versions.)

Costs

Design
You can create a catalogue with a software programme such as Microsoft Publisher or Serif Page. The great thing about doing it yourself (apart from the zero outlay) is that you can quickly modify

the saved document as a PDF file whenever you need to publish a new edition of your catalogue.

If you want to hire a designer to design a catalogue for you, you'll need to be sure that you'll have enough readers to justify the expense.

Printing

If you need to print your catalogue, you will need to explore the different paper, printing and binding costs. For small quantities, it is usually most cost effective to print them off on your office printer, but if you have a large number of catalogues with many pages, it will probably be better to go to a professional printer. The quality of the finished product may be the deciding factor though, as there is no point in producing a catalogue that looks unprofessional, as it won't sell your products.

Distribution

The method you use to distribute your catalogue can have a significant impact on your expenditure. Emailing the catalogue to your mailing list or offering it for download via your website is free, and it gives customers the choice of printing it themselves if they want to. If you decide to post out your catalogue, the cost can be astronomical, and that's before you've sent them to any customers overseas.

If you have an in-store catalogue that is never removed (as in Argos stores) the costs won't be too high as it is something you can produce on your office PC.

Mailing List

Established businesses that have a customer database will obviously have less trouble distributing an e-catalogue than new businesses that may have to buy a mailing list or wait to build a customer base.

Competition

A catalogue can be a useful tool that continues to sell your products outside of opening hours, away from your shop or stall. Because very few pet product retailers offer a catalogue alongside their other channels, gaining a competitive advantage in this way is easy. They can provide an advantage during working hours too. At an event or in a shop you may be limited by space, but with a catalogue you can offer a much wider product range than competitors with the same or larger floor space.

Profitability

Mail order is not one of the most popular ways of buying pet products, but it can be used to facilitate and capture extra sales that you would ordinarily miss out on because a customer either prefers to shop offline or has little time to visit your shop.

The cost of launching a mail order channel can be huge, particularly if you choose to print and post the catalogues. You will need to be sure that you have a big enough demand in order to recoup these costs and start making a profit. Creating an e-catalogue rather than hard copies will greatly reduce your costs.

Having an in-store catalogue that features a wider range than your shop, or your least popular products, can help improve your cash flow by reducing the amount of money you have tied up in stock.

Sometimes, it can be difficult to measure the revenue contribution of a catalogue since customers may consult one during the buying process, but then order via another medium such as online or by phone. One way to keep track of its success rate is to include a discount code with your catalogue, which incidentally is likely to have the added benefit of generating further catalogue sales.

Sales Channels: Direct Selling

For a long time, direct selling was the realm of Tupperware, Avon, and window sales reps. Today, direct sellers showcase all manner of products, including pet accessories, to people in their homes and workplaces.

Direct selling via home parties, a travelling shop, a drop-off box, and door-to-door, can be a highly fulfilling and lucrative method of retailing pet accessories.

This sales channel can help you establish yourself within your community and allow you to 'cross-sell' if you have other business activities aside from retail. Moreover, if you have produced your own range of products, but are struggling to get retailers to stock them, then direct selling may be the best method of distribution.

Home Parties

The home party is an ever-growing retail channel, which enables the seller to demonstrate and promote products in someone else's home or other location. The guests, plied with a glass of wine and in familiar company, are usually in a receptive frame of mind to buy.

To be a good home party host, you will need to be confident when talking to small groups of people and passionate about pet products. You don't have to be a hard seller, in fact, it is a bonus if you are not because guests will warm to you better and buy more.

If you are promoting pet products, it is highly likely that some of your party guests will have four legs, so you will need to be able to interact with animals and provide entertainment for them as part of your sales tactics.

Door-to-Door

Going door-to-door can be a soul-destroying activity and is seldom welcome by the home occupiers. The method may work well for window sales reps; after all, everyone has windows. Not every household has a pet though, and the value of any sale will be tiny in comparison anyway. (Although, if prospects can book an appointment with you online or by phone, your success rate may be much higher.)

However, you can still have great success selling door-to-door, not necessarily in residential areas, but in places where there are groups of people, such as business addresses, and community and social groups.

The Drop-off Box

The drop-off box is a method of direct selling that has been used successfully by gift and confectionery companies for many years. By putting a selection of pet products in a box, and then leaving it at a company (providing they agree), you can reach workers who may struggle to find the time to shop for their pet. Furthermore, your products can be a welcome distraction in an office, or staff canteen, and once one person has placed an order it will motivate their colleagues to buy. After about a week, you can then go back and collect the products and, hopefully, plenty of orders (especially if you have timed the box to coincide with their payday!)

The Travelling Shop

Loading up a van with products and visiting locations regularly is another way you can tap into this growing avenue. You could visit a dog-training centre, a cat competition venue, or a village square. Van sales can work particularly well in remote areas where the only other choices that customers may have are to buy pet accessories online or to travel thirty miles to the nearest pet shop.

The travelling shop is different from attending events, as it involves building a customer base, and increasing that base by word of mouth and other advertising methods.

Customer Expectations

Other sales channels can lack the personal interaction that customers receive from direct sellers. Direct selling offers the customer an alternative, more entertaining, sociable shopping experience, and this is what customers expect when they attend home parties or visit a travelling shop. You'll need a lively outgoing personality to be able to sell face-to-face, or to persuade organisations to accept your drop-off box.

Customers want to have enough time to look at the products, but you should not give them so much time that they change their mind about placing an order, which can be a risk if you take the drop-off box option. You should deliver products as soon as possible after a customer has placed an order, as you need to provide the same level of service as competitors and the other sales channels that you operate.

Customers will expect you to visit regularly throughout the year with new products. If you are a party seller, they will expect a different sales presentation and different activities for their pets each time.

Whatever approach you use, customers like to have your full contact details in case there is a problem, or if they need to re-order before your next visit, so business cards or other marketing materials are essential.

Costs

Advertising
For door-to-door and drop-off box selling, advertising won't be necessary, but for the party planner, some sort of publicity will be crucial. Spreading the word to generate bookings doesn't have to be a major cost if you can take advantage of social networking and other cheap advertising methods. (More on this in Chapters 7 and 8.)

You will probably need a vehicle to run this sales channel, which you can turn into an advert with some decals, and this will give your business a professional appearance.

Travel
Travel costs can be high depending on the locations you choose to host parties or visit businesses and groups. An unsuccessful party or drop off box can be costly if you have travelled a long way. Vehicle maintenance and repairs will add to your costs.

Delivery

You need to think about how you will deliver items to the consumer if you don't have the products with you when you accept orders. Delivering orders in your own vehicle will be cost effective in your local area, but you might want to consider posting or using a courier for delivering to customers further afield.

Marketing Materials

Most methods of direct selling will require order forms and price lists. You may also need brochures, and to provide your host with invitations for their guests if you are running home parties. Even if you are selling face-to-face, customers will probably like to have a receipt as well as details of how to contact you if they have a problem or need to make a repeat purchase.

Wastage

Inevitably, there will be some damage if you are displaying products in a drop-off box or allowing customers to try products on their pets at home parties. Wastage is a legitimate cost that you need to accept before starting up a direct sales channel.

Competition

Out of all the channels your competitors can use, home parties can be the most enjoyable and fun setting for shopping. Opportunely, most pet accessory companies don't utilise this method enough, if at all.

At home parties your products will be the only available, and unless guests use their smart phones during the party to compare prices, there will be no competition. With the drop-off box method, you may have a little more competition since you'll need to give the workers at least a few days to place their orders, in which time they could check online stores, pet shops, and supermarkets.

Profitability

The start-up costs are relatively small for direct selling, but it can be a hit and miss enterprise. Van and home party sellers can struggle to make a profit at certain gatherings, while drop-off boxes may not generate orders at some companies and social groups. Research is critical, as you will need to choose locations that will be lucrative so that you can recoup your ongoing costs such as fuel.

The biggest advantage is that out of all of the channels, direct selling offers the customer the most convenience. A travelling shop can become a profitable and valuable service within a community, especially if you purvey essentials such as pet food and health products, in addition to practical items and luxuries.

Your revenue from door-to-door sales will be higher if prospective customers request a visit from you, rather than cold-calling them, although some customers will feel obliged to buy whether you have an appointment or not.

Many workers feel guilty about leaving their pets at home all day, so gifts and impulse buys will be profitable additions to a drop-off box. If you operate near a commercial district, the drop-off method may not only be lucrative, but it may be a chance to promote your other business activities to further increase profit. Joining forces with another pet business, and then promoting both businesses together is also a great way to spread the word and promote sales.

Whatever method(s) you choose, reassuring customers that you are a genuine and trustworthy business will be key to your profitability.

Sales Channels: Events

Selling at events is no ordinary sales channel. It can be the sole channel for a full- or part-time business, part of a multi-channel strategy, or as a marketing strategy to raise brand-awareness.

The term 'events' covers so many possibilities. You can exhibit at specific pet shows such as Crufts, LovePets, London Pet Show, Discover Cats, and Discover Dogs, or general events such as county shows, gift and craft events, flower shows, markets, local bring and buy sales, and school fetes. You can choose to exhibit locally, nationally, or even internationally.

It is the flexibility of this channel that is particularly appealing, as you can choose exactly when, where, and how often to exhibit. It is also a great way to meet the customers and do some competitor-research at the same time. Don't assume though that it's easy money; there are often long days spent on your feet, hours of preparation, and for some, cold nights sleeping in their van.

Costs

Stand Hire

Generally, the larger and more popular an event, the more expensive the square metres will be to hire. This should not deter you from selling at big events though. Quite often, the high footfall and the quality of visitor will ensure that you get a good return on your investment.

In contrast, hiring a stand at smaller, local events may cost just a few pounds, and some may even be free, but you need to be sure that there will be enough people through the doors willing to buy your products. Smaller events are a good way to learn the ropes and the right ones will reap a good financial reward for you as well.

To reduce stand hire costs you should consider joining forces with another business, although preferably one not retailing pet products.

Exhibition Display & Signage

Some events, such as those that take place in church halls and schools, may provide a table gratis for you to display your wares, in which case you may only need to invest in a fabric table covering and perhaps some professional banners depicting your brand. However, most event organisers hire out a space and nothing more, leaving you to dress up your designated exhibition area from scratch. If you are on a budget, and faced with trying to compete with your rivals' professionally customised displays, then you may need to rely on some creativity to help your stand to stand out.

If you can design, transport, and erect the stand at the venue your-self, this will keep your costs down. However, at some point you may also need to hire an exhibition contractor or borrow a few willing friends.

Travel Costs

Whether you decide to exhibit locally, nationally, or internationally, there will be travel expenses involved. Obviously, the further away an event, the higher these costs are likely to be.

The one thing every exhibitor needs is a vehicle that is big enough to carry all of the stock needed, as well as any display equipment. Whether you have your own van, or borrow or hire one, remember that any costs such as fuel, insurance, and maintenance, all need to be recuperated before you can break even.

Accommodation

If an event is being run over more than one day, or if it is too far away for you to drive back at the end of the night, then you'll need to arrange accommodation. The organiser of an event can usually provide a list of local hotels and B&B's, and some establishments will offer discounts to visitors and exhibitors. However, many exhibitors would rather spend one or two uncomfortable nights sleeping in their vehicle rather than have yet another expense to eat into their profit.

Marketing Materials

Marketing materials, such as business cards and flyers, help to reassure prospective customers that you are genuine and that they can get in touch with you if there is a problem. By providing your details on a leaflet, you can also capture sales from customers who may need to take their pet's measurements, or research your business further before they buy.

Staff

At exhibitions, the flow of visitors can undulate. One minute there could be nobody in sight because everyone is watching a demonstration, the next minute there may be a crowd around you. At small events, you will probably be able to deal with visitors single-handed without losing many potential customers. However, at larger events you may need more staff to capture the attention of as many visitors as possible. If you have to hire extra staff for an event, you should make sure that they have prior event-experience and understand the products they are selling.

Following-up Leads

Following up enquiries with mail-shots or phone calls, within a week of an event will incur further costs, but the rewards can be high. Just by making contact you will be ahead of your competitors, as many never use the customer details they gather at events, and those that do, leave it so long that the visitors have forgotten all about them.

Customer Expectations

Many people visit exhibition shows looking for ideas and solutions, to be entertained, to learn something new, or to be the first to see an innovative product. Those that attend with the principal intention of shopping are obviously easier to sell to, but you can still capture sales from those that haven't considered opening their purses, by fulfilling or exceeding their expectations. At a gift fair, customers will expect to see gift products. At other events they might expect to see innovative and practical products. You should therefore adapt your product offering to suit the event and match visitor expectations.

Preparation is key. Prices should be clearly marked on every product to save you from having to repeatedly answer the same question, 'How much is this?' and to avoid losing customers that don't like to ask. Visitors may have questions about your products, or may seek your advice about pet related problems, and will expect you and your staff to be knowledgeable.

Competition

The level of competition you encounter will depend largely on the type of events that you select. At a pet-specific event such as Crufts or Discover Cats, all of the other stands will be pet-related and therefore competition will be intense. At general events, your competitors will all be vying for visitors' attention, and although not every visitor will be a potential customer, you may be the only stand selling pet accessories.

Exhibitors are facing competition from the internet, with visitors using smart phones to help them work out the best deal.

The location of your stand within a venue is an important factor in your competitiveness. Visitors might spot something they want to buy within minutes of entering an exhibition hall, but be reluctant to buy it in case they see something better at another stand. However, by the time they reach the exit, they may have run out of money. The exception to this is the permanent market pitch, where it can be an advantage to be in a prominent position, near the entrance, where customers know where to find you. By signing up to an event early, you may have more choice in the location of your stand.

Friendly staff that are approachable and actively engage with potential customers will do better than stalls whose staff allow customers to walk past.

Profitability

Due to the cost of exhibition displays, the initial investment needed can be high. You may be able to break-even and make a good profit after one big pet event, but attending shows regularly may be the only way to ensure that this sales channel is worth the initial preparation and effort.

Ongoing costs such as fuel can diminish any revenue you generate, so selecting the right event is crucial. Your primary research is an important starting point because it should identify the events that your target market are likely to visit, and how much they are likely to spend. You should then research the actual events because there are certain factors that will affect visitor numbers and sales. An entry fee might limit visitor numbers, but it ensures that the people who visit are genuinely interested in the event and are willing to spend money. In contrast, a free event may attract people who are just looking for a day out and have no intention of spending money.

The type of event that you stand at, whether general or pet-specific, will affect the quality of the visitor you encounter and thus the volume of sales. Where and how the organisers are publicising the event may give you an idea of whether enough people from your target market will be attending. A final clue about an event's potential profitability may come from finding out the events that your competitors are attending or not re-attending, as the case may be.

In the next chapter, we will discover the importance of creating a strong brand identity, and how the right branding can help attract more customers.

Branding and Brands

Business experts often talk about brands and branding as if they are the same thing. While the two are related, they are very different.

Branding is the collection of unique visual identifiers (such as your logo and colourway) that makes your business attractive and instantly recognisable. Your brand, on the other hand, is your business' personality, and is based largely on how the public perceive your company.

A customer will always choose a business with attractive branding and a consistent brand, over a business that doesn't appear to have invested much time or thought into it. Poorly executed branding not only makes a business and its products look unappealing, it may raise questions in the customers mind about what other areas of the business may be poorly implemented.

Developing Your Branding

I f you are a start-up business, then you are in the advantageous position of being able to look at the whole picture before you go ahead and brief a graphic designer or get ten thousand flyers printed.

Figure 4.1 How Branding is Developed

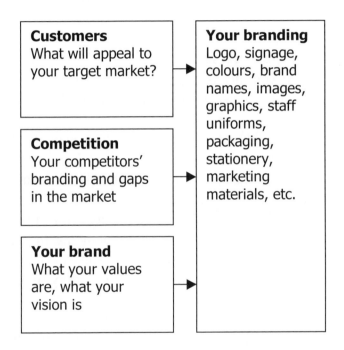

Figure 4.1 above shows that customers, the competition and your brand, play a huge part in developing your branding. Exploring each one will help you decide how your branding should look.

Customers

When it comes to designing branding, the most important thing you need to consider is what will appeal to your customers. You may have to make a few assumptions about the designs that will resonate with them, but this should always be based on your own market research findings. Factors such as age, income, occupation, lifestyle, education, religion, and location, can affect how your target market responds to your branding.

Age and Family Life Cycle

It is important to consider the ages of your target market and their current stage in the life cycle, as this will affect what branding will work best.

Young couples with no children, for example, may like the idea of freedom, spending weekends outdoors with their dogs, and having fun with friends. Therefore, pet companies with cool and trendy branding may appeal to them.

For couples with young children, the pet becomes an integral part of the family, and therefore, a company's branding that is family-orientated and gives the impression that its products can make their lives easier will have the most impact. Alternatively, branding that strikes a chord with the children, such as a caricature logo, a catchy tagline and bright colours will help encourage pester power.

In households with no children, pets sometimes become a substitute for children, so branding that reflects the central role that pets have in their owners' lives will have the most appeal.

Income

The average income of your target customers (their job title can give you a clue) is an important consideration when planning your branding. Upmarket branding that suggests your products and prices are above a customer's budget can be off-putting, although, it can increase desirability for those products. Similarly, if your target market is earning above a certain income level they might view a discounted 'cheap and cheerful' style as a step backwards.

Gender

The gender of your target market may affect elements of your branding. If your target market is principally one gender, then you can create highly focused branding that will appeal to them. Females generally prefer softer lines and colours, whilst males prefer styles that are more masculine and darker colours. If your target market is made up equally of both genders, then you may want to choose a more gender-neutral colour scheme for your branding. Of course, these are not steadfast rules, and you should be careful not to stereo-type.

Geographical Location

The sales channels you operate through will largely determine the geographical locations you target. Your business can be local (e.g., a stall at a local gala) or have a much broader reach (e.g., an online shop), or be somewhere in between.

If your target market is mostly 'local' i.e., they reside or work within one area, city or county, they may appreciate a reference to the locale in the brand name, or the inclusion of a local landmark in the logo. However, the owners of businesses that have a wider reach, such as internet shops, will need to do their research, as some colours or symbols may be seen as unlucky or offensive in certain cultures. A local reference or a play on words, such as 'The Isle of Cats', which requires special knowledge to be understood, could confuse a customer from another country, so unless it is world-renowned, exercise caution.

Behaviour & Lifestyle

The way in which people use products and their attitudes towards them, can vary. In the pet retail market, there are customers who believe that accessories should be purely practical and conservative in design, while for others the emphasis needs to be on style and fashion (although this group will still expect products to meet their practical expectations.)

The target market's lifestyle is another factor. Customers that work all day, or have hobbies and pastimes that do not involve their pets, won't be attracted to a brand that makes them feel guilty for not putting their pets in a more central role in the lives. In contrast, owners who spend lots of time with their pet will expect your branding to reflect this.

Competition

Branding helps to create a desired perception of a business, its products, and people, and reassure customers you have the same qualifications and abilities as all your competitors.

In your market research, you should have examined the branding that your competitors use to attract the same or similar markets that you would like to target. The colours, logos, imagery, themes and styles used by your rivals to appeal to customers, may give you ideas for the look and feel of your own branding. However, it is more important that you find any gaps that competitors have left. Anything that helps you stand out from the rest and attract customers will ultimately increase your profit. Perhaps there is a colourway that is currently not in use, or perhaps your competitors all share a similar theme, and there is, therefore, a gap for something very different.

In certain saturated markets, it may be quite difficult to find a gap. However, there could still be an opportunity to differentiate your business by taking a concept that is already in use and executing it better. Maybe one of your rivals has a 'Hollywood Glamour' theme, but they have not been consistent with it. If you run a dog hydrotherapy business or a cat hotel, for example, you could think 'spa retreat' instead, and repackage your offering as a relaxing, de-stressing experience for four-legged guests.

Your competitors' weaknesses are an opportunity to distinguish your business by building a stronger identity through your branding. Be aware though that some gaps in the market may have been left for a reason; they just don't work.

Your Brand

Although your logo, colour scheme, and tagline can give potential customers an idea of what to expect from your business, your brand is so much more than graphic design. After all, a logo is just a symbol, a colour scheme is a few colours put together, and a tagline is some memorable words that sum up what you do.

According to the Design Council, a brand is a set of associations that people make with a company, product, service, or individual. It is all the thoughts, ideas, feelings, and opinions that people have, which may be based on their previous experiences of doing business with you, the impression they get from your branding, or what their friends have told them. To be concise, it is your business' personality.

Your past and existing customers will have formed their opinions about your business based on key aspects, such as your customer service, product knowledge, quality, convenience, ease of ordering, delivery, interior of shop, and look of your website.

Prospective customers that have no previous experience of doing business with you, will base their decision about whether to buy your products purely on external information, such as word of mouth recommendations, and customer review sites, as well as the first impression they get from your branding.

As we will discover in Chapter 7, by delivering excellence in the areas that are important to your customers, you can create a positive association with your brand, and therefore positively influence what your customers tell their friends and family, or what they submit to the world on customer review sites.

Defining Your Brand

To define your brand:

1. **List the characteristics of your products and services.** (E.g., glamorous, stylish, innovative, pretty, value, fun, unique.)
2. **List the aims and values of your business.** (E.g., to bring affordable pet fashion to the UK. To improve the health and wellbeing of dogs in your local area with your products and services.)
3. **Define your target market.** (E.g., age, lifestyle, jobs, income.)
4. **What is your specialist area?** (E.g., small breeds, cats-only, improving dog behaviour.)
5. **How do you want people to perceive your business?** (E.g., as a business that values its customers, is ethical, loves animals, is energetic and different.)

Once you have your brand concept on paper, you need to refer to it every time you are planning business communications such as:

- Creating business cards and flyers
- Designing the look and layout of premises
- Writing content for a website or blog
- Designing signage
- Updating your Facebook page or Twitter account
- Answering the phone
- Talking to your staff
- Sending emails to your customers
- Writing an advert for Google Adwords

Ask yourself if your brand were a person how would it approach the various tasks of your business? How would it address its customers? (Formal or informal?) What language and tone would it use? (Energetic, fun, humorous, professional?) This will help you achieve a strong and consistent brand throughout your company.

External Brand Perceptions

You can heavily influence the perception of your brand by striving for excellence in the areas that your customers value, such as service.

However, there are always going to be some things that are out of your control. For example, a story could appear in a national newspaper concluding that dressing up dogs is cruel. While the story might not actually mention your business, it might get the general public questioning whether it is right to buy dog clothes, and this may have a negative, albeit indirect, impact on your brand. Similarly, a company's product recall could have an effect on every other business within the industry. For instance, a brand of cat treats may be recalled, and this may cause your customers to avoid buying all cat treats, even if you stock a different brand.

Thankfully, the effects of bad press are mostly only temporary, and the chances of a full recovery are vastly improved if you have already established a strong, positive association with your brand. However, a consistent run of poor reviews and complaints over a period of time can cause irreparable damage to a brand. This is why some companies spend thousands on re-branding; it wipes the slate clean enabling them to move forward and rebuild a new, more positive brand. The majority of small to medium businesses however, don't have thousands of pounds to spare if something goes wrong, so managing and maintaining your brand image will help you avoid costly re-branding exercises.

Branding

B randing is all the visual elements that make your business unique, and includes your logo, business and brand names, theme and style, signage, staff uniforms, packaging, stationery and marketing materials, images and graphics. If implemented well, your branding will give prospective customers a clear and immediate message about who you are, what you do, and what they can expect from you in terms of quality and service. It can also provide you with a competitive advantage, as it communicates what is different about your business, products, and services.

Branding helps to:

- Attract your target market
- Make your business look trustworthy and professional
- Appeal to your customers on an emotional level
- Represent your business' personality

- Increase desirability for your products and services
- Motivate customers to buy
- Make your business stand out from the competition
- Make your business instantly recognisable

For new businesses that are yet to build a customer base, branding is of vital importance because prospective customers will have nothing else to go on apart from their first impressions.

Choosing a Name

Your business name is possibly the most essential aspect of any branding. If you already have a business, but think your company name won't translate well to retail, then you may want to consider choosing a different brand name for your products.

Some of the best business and brand names are descriptive, (e.g., 'pet boutique' and 'doggy day care.') Although abstract and made-up names can work, it does make it harder to convey to people exactly what you do. Having an explanatory name is a bonus on the internet, as web addresses with good descriptive keywords will rank higher on search results pages.

Don't limit yourself by being over-descriptive. For instance, you may initially plan to supply dog-only products and give yourself the name 'Dapper Dogs Togs', but this may make it difficult for you to move into other areas such as cat and small animal products in the future.

As mentioned earlier, you can take inspiration from local land-marks or culture, if you think it will appeal to your target market, although you should be careful not to exclude potential customers from outside your territory.

The main issue is whether a name is already in use. You should search the WHOIS directory to see if anyone has registered the domain name. Check social networking sites such as Twitter (you may not plan to use such sites, but if someone else is using your name it may cause confusion amongst customers). You should also check if a name has been trademarked at ipo.gov.uk.

Once you have shortlisted a few names you should consider how a name will look in a logo or shop sign, whether it is easy to spell and whether it gives the right impression. As with most aspects of your business, you should ask the opinions of those that matter: your customers and staff.

Graphic Design

A major element of branding is graphic design. If you or a friend has an eye for design and a good grasp of software such as Photoshop or PagePlus, then you can produce logos and banners in-house. Being able to create your own graphics can reap considerable savings and it means you can also update your branding instantly whenever you need to without the need to hire a designer every time.

Whether you design your own branding or hire a graphic designer to do it, you should start with the design brief outlining what your vision for your brand is, who your customers are, and what image you want the branding to communicate to the public.

Often the hardest aspect of developing branding is not the designing, but translating your vision and values into something that is tangible, such as a logo or a staff uniform. Once you have come up with a few possible designs, it is a good idea to seek the opinion of your sample again, to find out which designs they like and they think work best, and what impression each gives about your business. It may take a few trips back and forth between your sample and the drawing board before you get it right, but it will be worth the effort.

Branding Evolution

E stablished businesses may find that their branding is no longer unique because competitors that have since entered the market have 'gained inspiration' from some part of their identity. Other businesses may feel that their logos have become outdated since they started up. If either or both has happened to you, there is no reason why you can't make subtle updates to your existing branding to stay one step ahead of rivals and stay on trend. After all, some of the most iconic logos have gone through several evolutions over time, and have often ended up looking very different from their original insignia. A branding update can give a boost to customers, staff, and owners.

In the next chapter, we will look at the various pet products available in the market, the best places to find reliable suppliers, and how to reduce the risks when importing.

Sourcing Products and Suppliers

Sourcing quality products from trustworthy suppliers can be an arduous task that requires much research.

When sourcing, it is important to keep in mind your overall aim; that you are looking for products that your customers want to buy, which you can sell at a profit.

Having a clear idea of the products that you need to stock, will make searching for suppliers easier. You can narrow down your search further by supplier type (e.g., manufacturer or wholesaler,) and location (e.g., the UK or overseas,) to get enhanced results.

Sourcing from overseas brings many benefits, but you will need to be aware of the different payment methods and documentation required to import smoothly.

Once you have a list of potential suppliers that can provide you with the right products, you then need to decide with which of them you wish to do business. While there are great trade suppliers out there, there are also some unreliable, unscrupulous outfits that need to be avoided. Thankfully, the internet makes the task of researching and vetting suppliers easier and more effective than ever.

Products

B efore you start searching for suppliers, you need to decide what products you need to stock (Figure 5.1.) Your market research will tell you which animals you need to focus on and which categories or types of products to stock. Good research will also identify the requirements that customers have of products, (such as styles, colours, sizes, characteristics, and uses), which will not only ensure that the products you eventually purchase meet customer needs, but will help narrow down your search, too.

Searching for suppliers of 'dog beds', for example, will yield far too many results, but if you know that your target market take their dogs on country walks, you can assume that they will need 'washable dog beds,' and such specifics will enable you to find a supplier more quickly.

Suppliers

Types of Suppliers

The types of supplier you choose can affect minimum order quantities, lead times, and margins.

Manufacturers
Buying directly from the manufacturer is a future aim for many businesses, as unit costs are much lower when buying in bulk and you can cut out the middleman.

Figure 5.1 Product Requirements Table

Animal	Product Types	Requirements
Dog	Collars, leads, harnesses, muzzles, ID tags, charms, jewellery, toys, clothing, coats, housing, kennels, cages, door flaps, beds, bedding, food, treats, supplements, agility/ training aids, healthcare, hygiene products, grooming equipment, coat sprays, shampoos, fragrances, feeding bowls, carriers, travel accessories	What styles, characteristics, colours, and sizes are needed?
Cat	Collars, harnesses, leads, housing, beds, bedding, cat flaps, toys, food, treats, grooming equipment, supplements, healthcare, hygiene, feeding bowls, clothing, carriers, travel accessories.	Does the product need to be waterproof, blingy, brightly-coloured, British-made, organic, fashionable, or customisable?
Small Animal	Bedding, carriers, cages, hutches, housing, leads, harnesses, food, toys, treats, healthcare, grooming.	What are the current and future trends?
Fish	Tanks, lighting, fittings, fish food, plants, aerators, decorative ornaments, healthcare.	What level of quality does your target market require?
Reptile	Tanks, lighting, heating, toys, plants, food, supplements, litter, bedding	
Bird	Aviaries, cages, healthcare, toys, treats, food, baths, nesting boxes.	Do they need to meet any quality standards such as ISO?
Horse	Tack, rugs, blankets, saddle pads and numnahs, saddles, head collars, browbands, boots, food, supplements, grooming, toys, treats, healthcare.	

Manufacturers tend to impose high minimum order conditions, either as a monetary value, or as a minimum number of pieces. Purchasing from a manufacturer usually requires you to have sizeable storage space, and you will need to be sure that you can turn over high volumes quickly, otherwise you may encounter cash flow problems due to the amount of money tied up in stock.

If you have ideas or designs for your own products, then you will need to approach manufacturers.

Wholesalers

Wholesalers buy in bulk, usually from several manufacturers. They then break up the bulk, add their own profit, and sell on to retailers in much smaller quantities.

If you choose to buy your stock from wholesalers, you will probably be subject to minimum order quantities, (especially if it's your first order with a company,) although, these are likely to be considerably less than those imposed by manufacturers.

Drop-shippers

Drop-shipping is an option that allows businesses to sell without ever stocking a single product. It works by you promoting the drop-shipper's products on your website or in a catalogue. When your customer places an order, you then order the products from the drop-shipper, who then packs and dispatches them direct to your customer. Your profit is the difference between your selling price and the price you pay the drop-shipper, which typically is around 30% of the RRP. The advantages of this are clear; you have no money tied up in stock, and you can offer a complete range without having to find storage for lots of SKUs (Stock Keeping Units). This leaves you to focus on sales and marketing.

Independent Craftspeople

Businesses often overlook independent craftspeople as possible suppliers. The volumes that they are able to produce are obviously smaller than mass manufacturers, the production time can be much longer, and they are generally a more expensive option than larger suppliers are. However, the products they produce can be highly distinctive, customised, ethical, or local, for which many customers are willing to pay a premium.

Location of Suppliers

The location of your suppliers can affect delivery times, product quality, communication, conditions, and costs.

UK

The manufacturing industry has diminished in the UK, so the majority of suppliers you'll find will be wholesalers.

There are many advantages to buying from the UK rather than abroad, including faster lead times, straightforward communication, and cheaper delivery. However, you are more likely to find yourself selling exactly the same products as your rivals.

Overseas

Sourcing overseas opens up your choices so you can benefit from expertise, craftsmanship, and technology that may not be available domestically. Russia, the Far East, USA, China, Italy, Korea, and Thailand are just some of the countries you could look to for suppliers. Some countries are better at producing certain products than others, so do your research.

Using suppliers abroad may significantly reduce unit prices, but

Figure 5.2 The Pros and Cons of Supplier Location

	PROS	CONS
UK	Get stock quickly Cheaper delivery costs Payment is straightforward by card, Bacs, or cheque Easy to communicate with Easy to visit Easy to contact if there is a problem Covered by UK law Low minimum order as most UK suppliers are wholesalers	Unit prices are likely to be high UK suppliers can easily supply your rivals, which could drive down prices
EUROPE	Wider choice of products and suppliers You can sell different products to those that many of your rivals will be selling Fairly easy to visit. Prices may be lower than the UK. No import duty to pay within EU Trade Zone	The language barrier Currency exchange rates can affect prices Quality standards and working conditions are not always the same as the UK Delivery times are longer Import duty and extra paperwork (for countries not in the EU)
GLOBAL	Widest choice of products and suppliers Generally cheaper prices You can get your own designs manufactured more cheaply	The language barrier Currency exchange rates can affect prices Delivery times are longest Working conditions and quality standards abroad are not the same as in the UK Import duty and extra paperwork

import duty and shipping costs can sometimes cancel out any savings you make. The language barrier can be an issue too, but foreign suppliers that are serious about exporting will have a sales rep that speaks English.

Import Basics

One thing that puts many people off from importing, especially from outside the EU, is the thought of all the extra paperwork they'll have to do. However, it is rarely as difficult as people imagine. In fact, your supplier (the exporter) will have to do most of the work.

When importing by sea, you'll receive a notice of arrival. If the size of your goods is Less than a Container Load (LCL) then your cargo will arrive in a groupage container, be taken to a bonded warehouse, and given a unique consignment number (UCN).

The consignment will not be released until the goods have cleared customs and for this to happen you will need to provide the shipping company with the Commercial Invoice, Packing List, and Bill of Lading, (which should be provided by your supplier.)

You will also need to provide your VAT number. If you are not VAT registered, then you will need to obtain an EORI number (Economic Operator Registration and Identification).

Finally, you'll need to provide the ten-digit Commodity Code for your products, which you can find out at Gov.uk. The code dictates the amount of duty and VAT to be applied so it's always wise to check this before you commit, and have the funds available on arrival to avoid having to pay storage charges.

If you purchased the goods from your supplier Ex Works, then you are responsible for all delivery charges from their factory to yours.

Once you have paid the import duty and other charges to the shipping company, and the goods have been cleared by customs, your consignment will be delivered to you.

When importing by air, usually the courier will pay the import duty and VAT on your behalf, to avoid a delay at customs. You will then have to pay the charges before the goods will be delivered, or you will be invoiced for the import duty within thirty days.

Importing can be this straightforward, providing your supplier has presented all the necessary documentation including a Commercial Invoice stating the number of units and their value. You'll need a statement of valuation if you are importing goods that are worth more than £6500.

Payment Methods

Payment methods can be a little more complex than if you were buying from the UK. While some foreign suppliers may accept card payments, Western Union, and even PayPal, bank transfers are the most common. SWIFT, the bank transfer system, is used to send foreign currency transfers outside the UK. You can do this through your bank, (some will let you do it online) for a fee.

Payment Terms

There are some different terms that you may come across when paying for imported pet goods:

Letter of credit – is a form of guarantee with your bank instructing them to pay for the goods only when the supplier has produced the export documents. There is a fee for this, but it does offer protection against suppliers who do not deliver the goods.

Advance payment – is the most common payment term when importing goods, and requires you to pay for the goods in full before the supplier ships them. This method obviously carries a lot of risk for the buyer and none for the seller.

Open account trading – is basically a credit account whereby the supplier sends out the goods and the buyer pays within the agreed timeframe. Whilst this carries no risk to the buyer, it is risky for the supplier and hence is not a commonly used payment term. Open account is usually used when a reliable buyer needs a regular supply of stock.

Beginning Your Search

A good starting point when searching for suppliers is the internet. A basic search might produce a substantial number of results, so be specific about what you are looking for, such as, 'pet bed wholesaler UK', or 'cat ID tag trade supplier', or 'designer dog products manufacturer China.'

Places to search for suppliers:

- Google search
- B2B Directories and Marketplaces (The Wholesaler, BT Tradespace, Alibaba, AliExpress, Global Sources, Busy Trade, Small Volume)
- Trade magazines and newspapers (such as Pet Product Marketing)
- Pet Trade shows (such as PATS in the UK, Interzoo in Germany, and Global Pet Expo in the USA)
- Cash and carries (such as Batleys and Makro.)
- Secret shopping (go into pet shops and make a note of the

distributor's address on the product price tags.)
- Online Communities such as wholesale and business forums, and LinkedIn may generate some possible suppliers.
- E-marketplaces (check the listings for wholesale job lots from liquidations and end of line ranges. In addition, some pet manufacturers sell direct to customers on e-marketplaces, so try contacting them to see if they will sell to you in bulk.)
- Sourcing or buying agents
- Networking events can uncover some great suppliers that your rivals may not be aware of, including local craftspeople

Approaching Suppliers

Your first contact with a potential supplier should be to determine if they have a minimum order and the prices they charge for their products. You should be brief and avoid negotiation until you have built up a rapport with a few emails, meetings, and phone calls.

Negotiation

It never hurts to ask a supplier if they can offer you a better price, or to suggest that one of their rivals has offered you a lower price, but that you are keen to do business with them instead. Telling them that you plan to place larger orders with them in the future can also encourage a reduced price, especially if it is your first order.

Shortlisting

While costs and quality are very important factors when sourcing products, there are other aspects such as reliability, ethics, and packaging to consider, which can help you to narrow down your search.

Capability and stability - Suppliers that have been operating for years will have learned from their early mistakes and become more efficient and competent. A financially stable company is more likely to make good on their promises. Above all else, a supplier needs to have the skills and experience to produce products to the quality and specifications you require.

How do they deal with defects? – At some point, you are bound to encounter a defective product. Will your supplier accept returns long after the initial sale?

Ethics and the environment – Increasingly, customers are becoming concerned about their carbon footprint. Ideally, you should try to source suppliers as close to you as possible to reduce any pre-purchase anxiety, although due to manufacturing capabilities in the UK this may be an unrealistic aim. Customers like to know that the products they buy have come from an ethical source where workers are treated fairly. Staff in countries such as China do not enjoy the same employment laws as their UK counterparts, so visiting factories to see the working conditions for yourself is recommended.

Don't put all your eggs in one dog basket – You should be seeking more than one supplier. If you rely on just one, and they unexpectedly close down, it could spell disaster for your business.

Your brand or theirs? – Selling products that belong to an established brand means that you can benefit from its reputation and marketing. However, if you would rather put effort into building your own brand than someone else's, then you have two options. You could choose a supplier that offers a white label service and have your logo imprinted on products. There is often a high minimum order imposed, which can make this option unviable to most small independents. Alternatively, you could source unbranded products from suppliers, and either just pass them off as your own or add your branded packaging, price tags, and labelling. Of course, the ultimate would be to design your own range of branded products. If this is what you plan to do, then you should ensure that suppliers have the expertise to handle the job.

Exclusivity – Having exclusive rights to sell a brand in your town, county, or country, is a coup for any business, although the supplier may demand higher prices, or that you meet criteria, in order to achieve this prestigious status.

Competition – You'll need to find out how many of your competitors are selling a supplier's products. A wholesaler selling direct to the public could pose a problem if they start lowering their retail prices.

Support – Do the suppliers offer point of sale materials, display units, and product information cards? Have they got a website or contact number for consumers, and will your details be added to their stockist information? Some suppliers will deal with your customers direct and replace faulty products or give them advice.

Discounts – Even if you are unable to negotiate a supplier down, you could still benefit from any discount and loyalty schemes they may offer. If you make frequent orders or spend high amounts, the savings you can benefit from in the long term can be better than a price reduction on your first order.

Terms – The suppliers' terms of sale, including lead times, prices, minimum order, and late delivery clause, should be compared to find the fairest suppliers.

Vetting Potential Suppliers

Before you go ahead and part with any cash, you should thoroughly research any prospective suppliers. Obviously, the bigger the purchase you are planning to make, the more time you should spend checking them out.

Google search – View their website or marketing literature to see what information you can glean. Check if they have genuine business premises rather than a mail-forwarding address. Read their company documents, which you can download from Companies House for a nominal fee.

Also, try Googling their company name, product, or brand along with 'complaints' or 'problems', to see if anyone has had issues with them in the past.

Visit them – Visit their premises, their stand at trade shows, or telephone them.

Ask for samples – If you are unable to visit, then ask for samples. You may have to pay for these, although some suppliers will refund the cost when you place a proper order.

Ask your target market – It is possible that some of your customers or potential customers will have encountered the products you are interested in stocking, so find out what they think about the brand by asking them in your primary research or via social networking sites, and by searching online review sites too.

Ask for references – Ask suppliers for a list of the people they supply, or look at their stockist's page and contact some of the businesses listed. You can also use business forums to ask if anyone has ever used a particular supplier, but be aware that by doing so you may be alerting rivals to a new supplier.

Consider supplier status and ratings – Some supplier directories and marketplaces such as Alibaba have their own vetting system, involving factory inspection and account auditing. However, a good rating doesn't mean you should automatically trust them.

Read the news – Search in trade magazines and business news for any evidence of financial problems within the company, such as redundancies.

Sourcing Agents

If you do not have the time to visit and vet suppliers, but want to rely on more than just a sample sent in the post before you place an order, then hiring a buying agent might be the answer. Sourcing or buying agents will visit potential suppliers to source products, collect samples, and negotiate prices on your behalf, as per your brief. Their hourly rates are often quite reasonable because they are not just sourcing for you; they are sourcing for other clients at the same time.

In the next chapter, we shall discover the pricing strategies and tactics you can use to gain a competitive advantage, and how to price your products to maximise your profit.

The Art and Science of Pricing

According to Prof Charles Toftoy, pricing is "part art and part science," and is arguably one of the hardest, yet most important tasks of any business.

It can affect how your brand and products are perceived, your sales volume, and ultimately your revenue and ability to survive.

If you pitch your prices too high, no one will buy. If you pitch them too low, you could be inundated with orders that leave you struggling to cope with a demand that brings very little profit in return. Furthermore, customers may question the quality of products that have price tags that are too good to be true.

There are a number of tactics and strategies that you can use when pricing, although, the majority of business owners don't consult a textbook when determining a price for their products. One 'scientific' method that will benefit businesses though, is the calculation of a price range rather than a single price. This can help you decide discounts, sale prices, as well as give you the flexibility to adjust and re-adjust the price to maximise your profit.

The Science of Pricing

B efore pricing products, business owners need to put aside the preconception that price can be used as a tool to compete. Yes, it is a factor that can influence buying decisions, but some independents become fixated on competing on price, particularly when they find themselves operating in the shadow of a big player, or when trying to gain market share amongst the countless online companies. They believe that customers are constantly seeking out the lowest prices, when, in truth, most are simply seeking *value* for money.

Benefits and Features

Although you wouldn't want to price yourself out of the market, it is important that your price reflects the benefits, features, and uniqueness of your product, such as:

- Quality workmanship
- Quality materials
- Durability
- Multi-features (e.g., the flexi lead that also dispenses disposable bags)
- Unique styles and designs
- Handmade, customised, or personalised
- British-made
- An exclusive brand

A price that does not reflect this *extra* may be dismissed by the consumer as being too good to be true and could have an impact on the overall perception of your brand.

Adding Value

You may want to consider the value you add in ways that have nothing to do with the product itself, such as:

- Your packaging and presentation (e.g., a gift wrapping service, gift boxes)
- Service (e.g., fast and efficient customer service, knowledge-able staff, a warm welcome and a free biscuit for four-legged visitors)
- A convenient location and an inviting shop interior
- Guarantees (e.g., free returns, extended exchange periods)
- Delivery (e.g., express home delivery, a gift sending service)
- Stocking a large or specialist range
- Credit terms

All of these factors have a value to the customer, which may be hard to define in monetary terms, but need to be considered all the same.

Pricing Strategies

There are a number of pricing strategies that you can use to help generate sales, depending on what you aim to achieve and your situation.

Prestige Pricing for Unique Businesses and Products

You can charge a higher price for products that are unique or exclusive, or if your location can justify inflated prices. For example, if you stock your own-design harnesses, are the sole company licensed to sell an innovative cat bowl, or yours is the only shop in a 30-mile radius that sells a particular brand, then you can charge a premium for your products.

Penetration Pricing for New Businesses and Products

Penetrative pricing is often implemented by start-ups to help establish themselves in the market. Products are initially priced low, but once a business has gained market share the price is increased. Consider this strategy carefully before you implement it because you can lose a significant number of your customer base when you hike up your prices.

Economy Pricing for 'Pile 'em High' Businesses

Economy pricing is the sort of strategy that supermarkets and multi-chain pet stores follow. The low prices reflect a product's low-cost mass manufacturing, and their often-tiny profit margins are viable only because they sell in such high volumes. Emulating such a pricing structure rarely works for smaller companies, and it is certainly not advisable to use an economy pricing strategy simply to compete with the big players.

Price Skimming for Niche Businesses

If you have a niche market, you can charge a high price because you have a competitive advantage. However, the advantage obtained from a successful niche is rarely sustainable. It doesn't take long before competitors notice that you're making lots of money and then start offering their own alternatives at better prices. By the time you have to lower your price for one product, you will hopefully have new niche product ready to launch at a premium price.

Pricing Tactics

Pricing tactics are textbook devices that you can employ to support your overall pricing strategy. Below are three of the most common.

Optional Extras Pricing

Businesses can try to increase their customer's basket value with 'price bundling' or optional extras pricing. If a customer buys a dog collar, for example, an optional extra could be a matching lead and an ID tag at a cheaper price than if they were buying the items separately.

Discriminatory Pricing

If you are planning to sell through more than one sales channel, you can use a discriminatory pricing strategy and charge different prices for the same product. Your shop, for instance, could be in a low-income area, but you may be able to sell at much higher prices from an exhibition stand at a pet show. Discriminatory pricing can also work within a single channel, such as by offering a reduced rate to students and pensioners.

However, keeping track of multiple retail prices can be tricky, and is usually not popular among the customers that miss out on the lower prices. To prevent such problems, you should provide clear information to the customer that they can get a product cheaper by purchasing through another of your channels.

Psychological Pricing

For many years, retailers have used psychological pricing tactics, such as £9.99 instead of £10, to convince buyers that a product isn't as expensive as it really is. Although this does work, increasingly consumers are becoming aware of such tactics and some studies suggest that rounding up prices may actually work better.

Price Setting

Price setting is a process of determining a price then monitoring the effects on sales volume and profit generation.

Price Data Gathering

Before settling on a price, you'll need to gather price information from various sources, including your target market, suppliers, and competitors. The best way to collect this data is to complete a table such as the one in Figure 6.1.

Figure 6.1 Price Data Gathering Form

	Product A	**Product B**
1. True unit cost	£	£
2. Your Bottom line	£	£
3. RRP	£	£
4. Competitors price	£	£
5. Minimum customers will pay	£	£
6. Maximum customers will pay	£	£

1. Calculate the True Unit Cost
Firstly, you'll need to calculate the true unit cost of each product:

Variable Costs
(The amount your supplier charged per unit including delivery, VAT, import duty, etc)

Fixed Costs
(Fixed costs such as rent & rates, utilities, labour, marketing, depreciation of fixed assets, etc, do not change with sales volume. To calculate these, you should add all overheads together and then divide by the number of units you expect to sell.)

2. Calculate Your Bottom Line (Cost Plus Pricing)

You should decide what profit you want to make on the product. By adding your profit to the true unit cost you should come up with your bottom line, or the lowest price you would be willing to sell the product for. In the past, businesses have used various methods for deciding their profit margins, including doubling or tripling the cost. However, ultimately only you can decide what would be a worthwhile margin and what will help you reach your revenue targets.

If you plan to run discount schemes and other margin-reducing promotions then you will need to cover this in the price or make it clear that sale items are not part of any discount offers.

3. Supplier Prices

Some suppliers provide RRP's (Recommended Retail Price,) SRPs (Suggested Retail Price,) or MRRP (Manufacturers Recommended Retail Price,) as a way of ensuring high profits for them and avoiding a price war amongst those that they supply.

However, RRPs are just that; recommended. In the UK, it is

illegal to enforce a minimum or maximum selling price on retailers. Furthermore, while some RRPs may be based on proven sales (i.e., the supplier has sold to consumers at that price, or someone they supply sells at that price,) sometimes the figures are simply plucked out of thin air. Therefore, prices suggested by suppliers should be viewed merely as another source of information to assist you in setting a price of your own choosing, and in some cases you should disregard this source altogether.

4. Competitors Prices

The price your competitors charge for the same or similar products can be used as a benchmark, providing the companies that you compare are similar to yours, e.g., in a similar location with a similar or the same target market. Before you take a competitor's prices at face value though, you should research exactly what their offer is. They may have low prices, for example, but charge the earth for postage, or a product of theirs may have a top price, but they may be yet to sell their first unit. You should take into account any regional price differences, too.

Compare how both you and your competitors add value. Whose offer is the most attractive to customers? What extra benefits and features do you provide? If your competitors do anything better than you, you may have to pitch your prices a little lower than theirs.

5. Minimum Customers are Willing to Pay

Business owners rarely consider the idea that a customer has a minimum price in mind. A minimum price is usually based on a customer's personal beliefs about how much they need to spend on a product for it to be of a satisfactory or desired quality. You can identify this price in your market research.

6. Maximum Customers are Willing to Pay

The maximum price your target market will pay for a product is down to their income, and other factors, such as how often they expect to use the product and how unique it is. You can identify this price in your market research.

Establishing a Price Range

Once you have filled in the table, you can look at the data to establish a price range for each SKU.

Identifying a price range rather than one single figure gives you the flexibility to adjust the price up or down whenever you need to without pricing out customers or making a loss. It also immediately flags up any products that you should discontinue or not buy in the first place because the profit they generate is lower than your bottom line.

The key data that you will need to compare are prices 2-6, with the most important prices being your bottom line and the price your target market is prepared to pay. The true unit cost only becomes important in situations where you need to sell off stock quickly, perhaps due to serious financial problems or low demand, as it will tell you the lowest price that you should charge to enable you to at least break-even.

The Rules:

1. Your price range should always be within the range that customers are prepared to pay.
2. The lowest price of your range should not be lower than your bottom line.
3. You should use RRP's and your competitor's prices as a benchmark only.

Figure 6.2 Example of Price Range Setting

	Product A	Product B	Product C
1. True unit cost	£0.87	£5.00	£11.50
2. Your Bottom line	£2.25	£10.50	£16.99
3. RRP	£3.99	n/a	£14.00
4. Competitors price	£3.99	£15.00	£14.95
5. Min customers will pay	£3.00	£10.00	£10.00
6. Max customers will pay	£4.50	£12.00	£15.00
Your Price Range	**£2.25 - £4.50**	**£10.50 - £12.00**	-

Product A – In an ideal world, your bottom line would be the lowest price, and the maximum that customers are willing to pay would be the highest, with the RRP and competitor's prices confirming that you are in the right range.

Product B – Most competitors will pitch their prices at the RRP if suppliers provide them, but if a competitor is successfully selling at a higher price, it suggests that there may be scope to sell at a high price too. However, it is the customer's budget that will ultimately determine the top price of your range.

Product C – The bottom line is higher than the maximum that customers will pay, and the RRP and competitors prices are lower than your bottom line. Unless you take a hit on your profit margin, Product C will not sell enough units at a good profit.

Setting a Starting Price

Setting a price will be relatively easy if a product has a narrow price range. A range could be so small that the only decision you have to make is a minor tactical one, such as whether to set the price at £10.99 or £11.00. If you have a much wider scope though, it is easy to get overwhelmed trying to decide whether to launch a product with a price at the top, middle, or lower end of its range. The price you start with will depend largely on your pricing strategy, (which we will look at more closely in chapter 9) and your revenue targets. However, it is not the launching price that is important ...

The Art of Pricing: Making Adjustments

The real art of pricing is not in the setting of a price, but in the evaluations and adjustments that you make to the price in the weeks, months, and even years afterwards.

Finding the Optimum Price

Businesses rarely get a price right the first time, so once you have a price range to work with, it is down to trial and error to find the price that will contribute the most revenue.

Lowering prices tends to increase sales volume and lower your profit margin, while raising prices generally decreases sales volume and increases profit margin. You also need to protect your brand image and avoid pricing out your customer base. You should therefore avoid making any sudden and substantial changes, and instead, make gradual adjustments and monitor the affects they have on sales volumes and revenue.

You will need to watch your competitors in case they respond with their own price changes.

Any changes you make need to be within your identified price range; never lower than your bottom line; never higher than what the customer is willing to pay and always at a level that provides a good profit.

The Continuous Process

As well as tweaking your prices in the weeks and months following a product's launch, you will need to continue to experiment with different pricing tactics in response to external changes. After all, the pet accessories market rarely stays static.

Economic fluctuations, changes in exchange rates, suppliers going bust, price wars, increasing admin costs, new competitors entering the market, and new laws, can all affect future sales of your products and require you to review your pricing methods. The weather can have an effect as well. For example, if you know that milder weather is around the corner following a cold snap you could generate some last minute sales of your winter dog coats by lowering their prices.

In the next chapter, we will look at how to attract customers to your business with the right advertising, and how to make the most of free publicity methods.

Attracting Customers

E verything so far has been geared towards creating the perfect proposition for your target market; from sourcing the products that they want to buy and setting the right prices, to choosing the best sales channels and designing a brand concept that gives your business desirability.

With the stage set, you now need to get customers through your doors and get them to buy. To do that you will need to raise awareness of, and attract people to, your pet accessories business, through advertising and publicity. Depending on the marketing options you choose, potentially this could be an extremely expensive exercise, so to avoid wiping out any profit you make, you should utilise the cheaper publicity methods as much as possible, and learn how to harness the power of free word of mouth advertising.

Attracting customers to your business is all about learning which methods work best; setting goals and evaluating is integral to this.

Advertising & Publicity Options

A dvertising and publicity are very different. Advertising is paid-for marketing over a set number of times, such as a classified ad that runs on a website for a month. In contrast, publicity can require a lot of creative thinking, but very little money.

As you will see below, there is a vast choice of marketing options available to use to get your message across to potential customers.

Advertising	**Publicity**
• Newspapers & magazines	• Pet shows & events
• Flyers and leaflets	• Seminars and talks
• Brochures	• Promotional giveaways
• Posters	• Sponsorship
• Inserts in newspapers	• Press releases
• Classified ads	• Networking
• Directories	• Company website
• Email marketing	• Window displays
• Pay Per Click advertising	• Video adverts & tutorials
• TV advertising	• Podcasts
• Radio advertising	• Competitions
• SMS text messaging	• Social network pages
• Telemarketing	• Newsletter & Blog
• Billboards & sign picketing	• Publicity stunts

Choosing the Right Options

Costs aside, it would be very easy to go through the above list and tick all of the options in order to maximise the number of potential customers you can reach. However, you need to research the effectiveness of each to avoid wasting time on mediums that won't help you connect with your target market, or won't provide a good return on your investment.

The permanence of marketing options can be an important factor. Setting up a fan page on Facebook, for example, can have a lasting effect, as the page will always exist. Moreover, with continuous input, more users will become fans of your business and the effect will spiral. In contrast, an advertisement in a weekly newspaper has a temporary effect, and will probably only generate sales during that week or until readers throw the paper in the bin.

Even if a marketing option is free and simple to set up, you'll need to consider the reputations of the 'locations' and advertising organisations with which you align yourself, as you wouldn't want your business to be associated with any negative or unsuitable publicity.

Reaching your Target Market

Your research findings should offer guidance on the best approach to promoting your business. For instance, if you know which magazines and websites your target market like, you could think about advertising in these, or if you know that prospects like to visit pet shows, you could consider taking a stand or giving a talk at one of the events that they attend.

You should also get into the habit of asking existing customers how they found you, to give you an idea of the best way to attract new customers.

The most important thing to consider is how many potential customers you will reach using a specific advertiser or medium. If you plan to advertise in a magazine or newspaper, then find out how many people read the publication (you can check the ABC circulation figures) and their readership demographics (most advertisers will provide this information.) If you plan to advertise on websites, use Alexa.com first to find out the site's ranking, traffic sources, and audience statistics for free.

It can be more difficult to estimate the effectiveness of publicity, such as a flash mob, especially if it's never been done before, as there are so many factors that could affect the result.

Attracting Customers on a Budget

T he cost of implementing marketing options can range from the very expensive (such as Television) to the free (such as writing a press release.) Your budget will ultimately dictate what you can and can't do to attract customers to your business. Fortunately, there are plenty of ways to achieve your aims without the need for an enormous marketing budget.

Organise an Event
Organising a group dog walk that meets outside your shop on a regular basis, or arranging a coffee morning (with biscuits for both owners and pets) will attract new people and is likely to increase revenue.

You should think about how you can use your professional skills and knowledge to create exciting events. You could teach pet owners how to check for mites, calm an aggressive pet, get a dog to stop pulling on the lead, make their own pet treats, cat toys, pet jewellery, etc. If you don't have any professional knowledge yourself, you could invite a guest speaker to do it instead.

Referral Schemes
If you have been trading for some time, you could try to increase your

customer base with a 'Recommend a Friend' scheme, whereby you offer a small incentive, such as a discount, to get your current customers to give you their friend's details (with their friend's permission of course.) Usually, you will need to offer an incentive to both your customer and their friend.

Social Petworking

Using social networking sites such as Facebook is a great way to raise awareness of your business. Your research should have identified whether your target market uses such sites, and therefore whether it would be worth setting up an account for your business.

Once up and running you can start by asking your friends and family to become a fan of your business, maybe launch a pet photo competition or run a new fan of the month contest. Many campaigns to increase fans can quickly snowball because people see their friends becoming fans and want to do the same. The result is you have a massive pool of potential customers to whom you can promote.

Furthermore, by setting up a page for your own pet (the face of your business perhaps?) and interacting with other 'pets' online, you can tap into the growing trend of 'social petworking' and the increasing number of pets that have an 'online presence.'

Offer Chances to Win Money-Can't-Buy Prizes

People love to win, so you could try launching a competition to get the public designing a new product, which you will produce and stock.

Publicity Stunts

One of the most bizarre things done to garner publicity for Prince & Princess Petwear was to create a dog collar with a built-in Rolex watch. It's a ridiculous, crazy concept; exactly the sort of story that the tabloids love. The Sun and The Daily Mail both ran the piece, and within hours, "The Watchdog" was being discussed on news sites and blogs all around the world. 'Prince & Princess Petwear' was Googled thousands of times by people checking to see if the story was actually true. Most importantly, traffic to the website, and sales, went through the roof.

Multinational companies pay huge sums for that kind of world-wide coverage, and we got it for free, just for coming up with a tabloid-friendly story. You too can come up with something that will get people talking by thinking outside the box, and brainstorming ideas for possible publicity stunts with your staff, family, friends, and customers.

News Stories

Of course, you don't have to churn out wacky ideas every time in order to get free publicity. If you can build a good relationship with your local newspaper by providing them with newsworthy stories, it should guarantee regular free publicity for your business. Possible newsworthy stories could cover anniversaries, launches and re-launches, winning an award, the 1000th customer through your doors, free giveaways or competitions for readers, charity fundraising events and interesting record attempts, or an exposé of the pet industry. If you have such a story, you should write a good press release and send it to the paper in the body of an email.

Free is the Magic word

FREE! Nothing grabs people's attention like the word 'free'. Every-one likes getting something for nothing; especially something of value to them. Think about what you can give to your customers that is of real value to them. Free reports, promo gifts, free prize draws, can all be offered in exchange for getting prospect's details such as email addresses which you can then use for future marketing campaigns.

Your Website: The Ultimate Advert

Whichever marketing options you choose, a web presence is a must for any business trading in the 21st Century. Whether you run a basic informational webpage or a full-blown ecommerce shop, a website is the ultimate advertisement, doing its job 24 hours a day, 365 days a year. Therefore, it needs to follow the rules of a good advert by ensuring each page is attractive, and gets its message across, whether it be; 'call us today'; 'buy now'; or 'sign up here'.

A website can provide a lot more information than the average advertisement, but as a bare minimum it should include details of who you are, what you do, your contact details, why you started up, and your mission statement. Of course, none of this matters if no one can find your site...

Increasing your Website's Visibility

There is no point investing lots of money and time in building a website, if no one can find it, which is why you need to be proactive in generating visitors, or 'traffic'.

Traffic to your website can come from the following sources:

Direct - People who reach your website by typing in your ULR, (or web address,) by clicking on a link in an email, or via a bookmark they have created, all form direct traffic. You can increase direct visitors by having your web address in as many places as possible, e.g., on all of your marketing materials, your vehicles, signage, staff uniforms, your email signature. Using a QR (Quick Response) code as well as the written address may further increase direct traffic.

Referrals – These come from links from other sites on the internet. You can increase links by adding your website's details to related online directories (start with ISEdb.com, which is a directory of directories, and work your way through the shopping and pet sites). Not only does building links send traffic straight to your website, they convince search engines such as Google that your website is popular and deserves a top ranking.

Links from your blog, Twitter, Facebook, and article submissions, can refer high volumes of traffic to your website, although banner ads, another type of referral, are very unpopular with internet users.

Search engines – The majority of visitors will arrive at a website through one of the big search engines such as Google, Yahoo, Ask, Bing, or Dogpile. Most people don't even scroll down the first page of results never mind click onto the second page. Therefore, if you don't appear at the top, you won't exist to the vast majority of people.

There are two ways to achieve a top ranking in the SERPS; paid-for advertising, which yields short-term results; and free organic search engine optimisation, which should eventually make up about 75% of the total traffic to your site.

Pay Per Click Advertising

You can instantly get to the top of SERPs with Pay Per Click (PPC) advertising from providers such as Google (Adwords) and Yahoo! (Search Marketing), providing you are willing to bid high enough per click.

To generate the right keywords, you will need to think about the products that you are selling, and the key phrases people will use to search for them. Google's Keyword Tool is invaluable, as it shows you the number of searches per month and the level of competition for keywords, and you can see what keywords your competitor's websites are targeting, too.

'Cat collar' may be too broad a term. 'Crystal cat collar' may narrow the results down, but still have a high level of competition. 'Breakaway crystal cat collar' may be relevant enough to get you a good SERPs position.

Many businesses believe that the aim of their Pay Per Click ad campaigns is to achieve a number one position. However, potential customers don't just accept the first result that Google gives them. Once they've had a look around the first website, they usually then back out of it to check the second and third results. If all websites are offering similar products at similar prices, will they then back out again and return to the first website? No, of course not, they will probably stay where they are and make a purchase or an enquiry. Therefore, you'll have much more success aiming for the rankings just below the top spot.

Search Engine Optimisation

The weeks and months following your launch may see your biggest online PPC expenditure as you try to increase traffic and generate sales. However, once people start to find your website naturally in the results pages, you can reduce your online advertising budget, and only increase it when you need to boost sales during quiet or competitive periods.

Achieving a high-ranking by organic means will take time, but you can make it happen by:

- Inserting relevant keywords and phrases in your meta data (title, meta description, meta keywords)
- Including keywords and phrases in your content, including at least 250 words of keyword-rich text on the homepage
- Ensuring all of your images have ALT tags
- Regularly updating your site by adding new content (e.g., a

blog)
- Using a domain name that has relevant keywords in it
- Improving your link popularity (see referrals, page 118)
- Reducing the number of outbound links (e.g., reciprocal links)
- Having a ULR that has been in existence for some time
- Adding a sitemap
- Having unique title tags for every page

If all this sounds like your worst nightmare, then it is probably a good idea to hire someone to optimise your site for you. SEO is an ongoing process, so if you can learn to do some of it yourself then you can save yourself a lot of money whilst also increasing your sales.

Recruiting Existing Customers

If you have an established business, you could recruit your existing customers to help you increase your customer base.

Reviews

One medium that is increasing in popularity is online reviews sites such as Reviewcentre.com, where customers can rate products and services. You can incentivise your existing customers to post reviews about your business, which will encourage new people to find out more about you and boost your profile.

Word of Mouth

Word of mouth advertising occurs when people talk about your business to their friends, family, work colleagues, neighbours, and even fellow dog owners in the park. Unfortunately, most people tend to tell others about a company or a product after they've had a bad experience. For them to make positive recommendations, it usually takes something exceptional.

Many business owners mistakenly believe that word of mouth advertising is something that they cannot influence. While it is impossible to control what people say to each other, you can create the WOW factor that will make customers want to tell their friends about you. In Chapter 8, we look in-depth at how to create exceptional customer service.

Setting Goals & Evaluating

Whether you want to increase sales, increase your customer base, raise awareness of your business, or get more people to sign up to your newsletter, you should have clear aims about what you want to achieve from each of the marketing options you select. By setting goals, you can review your marketing effort at regular intervals and, if necessary, make improvements or even stop a campaign if it is not accomplishing what you hoped it would.

Having the ability to track and monitor the results of your marketing is important if you want to find out what works and what doesn't. Monitoring your campaigns is easy if you use a unique promotional code in each of your adverts, or ask customers to quote a special reference when they get in touch. Google Analytics and WebTrends are great for tracking the response of campaigns, but if you use paper vouchers you will need to deal with these manually in order to find out the response rate.

If you get a good response from an ad campaign, such as an increase in website traffic or visitors to your boutique, but you don't achieve your primary goal of increased sales, then you will need to review your website, premises, and staff, to find out what is putting off potential customers. One common problem is when an advert gives a certain impression of your business that turns out to be unfounded. Your advertising and publicity must match your brand, otherwise it may be easy to attract prospects, but hard to convert them into paying customers.

If you don't get increased enquiries, orders, click-throughs, or impressions from a campaign, then it is the adverts themselves that are ineffective and you should re-examine the imagery, copy, and language used, and the places in which you have placed your adverts.

In the next chapter, we shall discuss how to keep the customers once you have attracted them to your business, through communication, rewards, and good customer service.

Keeping Customers

I t costs much less to retain existing customers than it does to attract new ones. Nevertheless, you would be surprised how many businesses spend time and money acquiring customers, only to neglect them in the pursuit of attracting more new customers.

However, just because a customer has bought from you in the past, it doesn't mean that they are loyal or that they will even remember you the next time they need to buy pet accessories. Most customers need some sort of regular reminder that you exist.

Keeping customers interested in what you do, thankfully, is much easier when you have their contact details, although you will need to be careful; no one likes to be bombarded with unwanted marketing.

Once you have earned a customer's loyalty you will need to reward them in order to retain them in the long-term. Rewards, however, do not have to cost you much for them to be effective.

Retaining Customers

Proactively retaining customers is something that all businesses must do to generate steady income. There are three things you can do to retain customers:

1. Be customer focused;
2. Communicate regularly;
3. Reward loyalty.

1. Be Customer Focused

A business that puts the customer at the centre of its operation will make customers feel good and encourage repeat sales.

New Products, Services, and Events

One way you can retain customers is by meeting their changing needs with new products and services. Not only does it show customers that their needs are important to you, it also makes them eager to return regularly to find out what new products they can buy.

Events such as coffee mornings, seminars, and dog walking meets, are a good excuse to get your customers to come back, and it demonstrates to them that you are more than just a retailer trying to make a profit.

Seek Customer Suggestions

By seeking the opinions of your existing customers, you can garner information about how to improve and grow your business, and you will show your customers that you are putting them, and their pets, at the heart of everything you do.

Exceptional Customer Service

You need to give customers a reason to buy from you rather than the competition. More often than not, your biggest opportunity to compete (especially with big players) will lie in your customer service. Therefore, if you can identify your competitors' weaknesses in this area, and then offer a superior service, you should be able to keep customers coming back to you.

Ways to create exceptional customer service include:

- Providing helpful, honest, and highly-knowledgeable sales assistance
- Treating the customer as an individual
- Caring for the customer by being courteous and attentive (think 'personal shopper')
- Connecting with customers and creating a rapport with them
- Offering innovative quality products
- Seeking to provide quality in everything you do
- Putting the customer at the centre of everything you do
- Keeping your promises

Complaint Handling

At some point, you will encounter a complaint from a customer. It could be because you sold them a product that has a defect or is the wrong size. Sometimes, it won't even be due to a failure on your part.

The great thing about receiving a complaint is that it is an opportunity to prove to the customer that you are trustworthy and professional. After all, until something goes wrong, they won't really know if they can trust you. If you can listen to the customer explaining the problem and focus on a satisfactory solution, you can win a customer's lifetime loyalty.

It is worth mentioning that not all customers are worth keeping. Some customers are a drain on your resources and bring in little revenue in return. Don't be afraid to let customers go, and cease marketing communications to them, if they persistently cause you problems.

2. Communicate Regularly

It can be a little unfair that customers who have had a good experience with your business can forget, while those who have encountered a problem seem to remember forever. Regular communication is the key to ensuring that the customers who love what you do receive reminders to buy from you again.

Permission Marketing

Before sending emails, mailings, or any other marketing communications to prospects, you will need to obtain their permission. Rather than this being something that restricts you though, it makes your marketing effort more effective as you focus only on the people who are receptive to what you have to say.

There are a number of ways you can obtain permission to contact customers. You could request their details in exchange for entry in a prize draw, or invite customers to sign up to your newsletter. If you run an online shop, an opt-in box during the checkout process can have a high success rate.

Obtaining consent is just one part of your task. Author and marketing guru, Seth Godin, said that permission marketing was a privilege given to businesses by customers, to deliver *relevant* communications. In other words, if a customer is only interested in products for cats, don't waste their time by sending them details of hamster products.

If you are unable to create different versions of an email or mail shot for each of your target groups (based on the type of pet, or price points, etc) then a general campaign that has something for everyone is the next best thing.

Whether you are able to send focused communications or not, you must make sure that you only contact prospects when you have something of value to say. Sending out a monthly marketing email because it is 'just something you do' is not a good enough reason for blocking up somebody's mailbox. At best, your recipients will start to delete your emails without reading then. At worse, they will request that you remove their details from your mailing list and you will have lost a potentially good contact. A new product line, a clearance sale, or a discount voucher, are good examples of what might be of value to your customers.

You need to protect your customer's data by keeping it secure, and only using it for the purposes for which they have agreed. Some organisations sell their marketing data to third parties, but buyers and sellers of this data forget that the most valuable aspect, the *permission* given by customers, cannot be transferred. Permission can give you an edge over the competition and generate repeat sales, so even if you have consent to sell data to third parties, don't.

Marketing Methods

You can use the same marketing options to attract customers (listed in Chapter 7) to try to retain them. However, some of the methods such as newspaper advertising can be expensive, and not a cost-effective method of keeping your existing customers updated. If you have your customer's permission to use their email address, postal address, or phone number, or they are following you on Facebook, then it makes sense to market directly to them using these methods.

Email Marketing

Email is an easy and effective way to keep in contact with your customers and anyone else that has subscribed to your marketing updates. Best of all, it is free.

You can send plain text emails to your mailing list, although the success rate tends to be higher if you send the more professional-looking HTML, newsletter-style emails via an e-marketing company such as Constant Contact or Mail Chimp. These software providers make it relatively simple to create different email campaigns for your different customer groups, too.

It can however, be all too easy to overuse this method, largely because it is free, but also because it allows you to communicate with an infinite number of people just with the press of the send button.

One obstacle to the effectiveness of email marketing is getting your message to stand out amongst all the other communications that your contacts receive. Although personalising emails with the recipient's name can improve your success.

Mailshots

You can keep in touch with customers by posting mailshots such as letters, leaflets, brochures, postcards, and invitations.

Mailshots are a good way to reach certain customer groups, such as the older generation, that perhaps won't respond well to electronic methods of marketing. Furthermore, if your competitors are relying solely on modern media to promote their business, it might be worth sending your customers a mailshot instead, just to differentiate yourself.

Increasing printing and postage costs, as well as design charges, can make this an expensive option, even when economies of scale apply (the more mailings you plan to send out, the cheaper each one will be.) There is also the environmental impact to consider.

Telephone Calls

Telephoning customers to keep them updated will guarantee that they personally receive your message, whether it is an invitation to an event, an update on the products they have been waiting for, or just a friendly hello. The fact that you have taken the time to call them will make them feel valued, and you could use the opportunity to do a bit of market research, too.

There are a few disadvantages though. If you have a large contact list, it could take a long time to call everyone, and your phone bill could skyrocket if some of your contacts are in a chatty mood when you ring. In contrast, calling at an inconvenient time can be detrimental to your campaign. Therefore, it is probably best to reserve this method for your best and most familiar customers. Being on familiar terms with your contacts means that you will know how to greet them and whether to take an informal or formal tone. Therefore, you should be able to get the most out of every call.

SMS Text Messaging

Unlike email, most people will read a text before they delete it. While you don't have as many characters in a text in which to bring about a call to action, busy people who are bombarded by marketing communications will definitely appreciate such brevity.

The increasing numbers of smart phones is great news for businesses that choose to market by SMS, as it means you can stimulate an immediate response from your recipients, such as getting them to visit your website or online booking page, or to phone you.

Obviously, you could send individual texts from a mobile phone handset, but if you are sending lots of messages, it will be more cost- and time-effective to use a text message provider, such as Text Marketer. Using such software will make it easier to target the different customer groups on your mailing list.

Social Networking

Using social networking sites, such as Facebook and Twitter, is different from other marketing methods. For a start, you don't need to obtain any personal contact details; you just need to get people to follow you. This tends to be an easier task if you have an existing online presence, because you can get people to click through to your social page via a link on your website or product listing.

Social networking sites are free to use, but you will need to update your followers regularly in order to keep them engaged. To be effective, your updates should try to encourage two-way communication as much as possible. For example, you could pose market research questions, debate relevant news stories, ask people to vote for brands that they would like you to stock, or simply interact with your followers.

If you have a big following, social networking can enable you to launch events, such as clearance sales, at very short notice because word will soon spread.

The major downside to this method is that you cannot target specific groups with tailored messages, so your updates need to appeal to all followers.

Public Relations

Public Relations, or PR, concerns all your business communications with the public and includes emails to customers, letters, advertisements, your website, blog and any articles written about you in the media. Good PR can help give you and your business credibility, build awareness of your brand, and present your business in the best possible light.

PR really comes into its own when things go wrong, such as in the event of a product recall. If managed correctly, PR can help to avert a crisis, limit damage to your brand image, and ensure that both potential and existing customers are not discouraged to buy from you in the future.

3. Rewards

We all know how it feels when a company you have been loyal to, entices new customers with great discounts and free gifts, whilst not rewarding its existing customers. By rewarding all customers equally, they will reward you with their loyalty.

Gold Card

Loyalty schemes are an effective way to encourage customers to keep returning. You could give customers reward points every time they shop with you, and they could earn gifts or vouchers when they've collected enough points. If customers are working towards a 'prize' from your business, they won't want to spend their money with your competitors.

You could give your best customers membership of a VIP club, and offer them privileges such as discount vouchers, special events, and free upgraded delivery. Customers that feel they belong to a special group are more likely to stay loyal.

Treat Customers like Friends

Sending your customers a Christmas and birthday card will make them feel part of the family. It is even better if you know the birthdays of their pets, so you cannot only impress customers by remembering, but you can use the opportunity to remind them in advance where they can buy their pet's birthday present!

As the owner of a pet business, you will often get to hear about your customers' pet-related problems, which can include behavioural and medical issues. Giving customers a courtesy call to find out how their pet got on at the vets, or if a product they bought from you solved their problem, will show them that you have been thinking of them and is a sure-fire way to impress them.

The Power of Free

As discussed in Chapter 7, giving something away for nothing such as a promotional gift or a written guide is a great incentive to get people through your doors and make a repeat purchase.

Enlist your Customers' Help

Everyone likes to feel needed. If you can get customers to help you in a small way, such as recommending you to their friends, liking you on Facebook, or offering you suggestions, they will feel that they are part of your business.

You could also involve your customers and their friends by launching a 'design a pet product competition' and getting the winning design produced, or getting customers to vote for products or brands that they would like you to stock. You don't always have to give away gifts and discounts to show your appreciation either. Saying thank you for their support is often enough of a reward.

If you have a customer that really loves what you do, then consider hiring them. Even if you are unable to offer them a full-time job, you could take advantage of their enthusiasm by getting them to host home parties, or hiring them to help you sell at events.

Mention their Name

Most customers love to see their name, or their pet's name, given a mention. There are probably plenty of opportunities within your business to do this. You could set up a photo gallery on your website, mention a competition winner's name on your blog or newsletter, or have a notice board with pet photos in your shop.

In the next chapter, we shall discover how you can use your financial records to make better business decisions, and how to troubleshoot financial problems when they arise.

Improving Your Financial Performance

Keeping accurate financial records is more than just a legal requirement. Your books, profit and loss account, and balance sheet provide the only true indicator of your business' well being; its profitability.

Unfortunately, these documents can only tell you what has happened in the past, when it may be too late to take action if there are issues. By re-arranging the data and collecting just a few additional statistics though, you can uncover the mine of information that is hiding in your financial books. If any problems do begin to arise, this data will enable you to immediately pinpoint the source (income, outgoings, or cash flow) and implement the correct solutions.

Keeping Records

Single or Double Entry Books?

Understandably, many business owners maintain just the bare minimum of records to limit the amount of time they have to spend poring over the figures. While basic, single-entry bookkeeping will satisfy the taxman, it won't really tell you much apart from what you earned and spent in a particular period.

Double-entry bookkeeping presents a breakdown of your incomings and outgoings, so you can see exactly how each area of your business is performing. [Download available at Elmsbury.com.]

Figure 9.1 Example of Purchases Book

Date	Details	Total	Ref	Stock	Rent	Legal	P+P
2.3.12	Mail Service	£9.67	001				£9.67
3.3.12	Supplier X	£76.00	002	£76.00			
3.3.12	AB Insurance	£8.00	003			£8.00	
4.3.12	Mail Service	£4.55	004				£4.55

Figure 9.2 Example: Sales Book

Date	Details	Total	Ref	Website	Parties	Shop
1.3.12	Wilkins, T.	£45.50	001	£45.50		
2.3.12	Clark, P	£23.99	002			£23.99
2.3.12	Johnson, S	£15.00	003	£15.00		
5.3.12	Ball, M	£160.00	004		£160.00	

Keeping Up To Date Books

Some owners are so busy with the day-to-day running of their business they struggle to find the time to maintain up-to-date records. However, if it's not a tax return that motivates business owners to get organised, then it's knowing that avoiding the books for too long can have serious financial repercussions.

Many EPoS systems and ecommerce solutions will record transactions as they occur, but when automation is not possible you'll need to update your books manually, preferably on a daily basis. Leaving your paperwork to pile up for more than a week can make it harder to start the task and longer to complete when you finally get around to it.

By bookkeeping little and often, you will spot the first warning signs of financial problems and be able to take any necessary action at the earliest opportunity. For example, if you have an online sales target of £2500 each month, but you only update your books once every fortnight, then it will be the middle of the month before you discover whether you are on course to meet that target. If things aren't going well, then you will only have two weeks to put it right.

Management Accounting: Uncovering your Books' Hidden Potential

By applying the current and historical data that you have from your double-entry books, and collecting some additional statistics, you can identify trends and patterns, and use them to make better decisions.

This data can help you to:

- Make decisions such as when and how much stock to purchase.
- Monitor the effects of price changes, promotions, marketing, and external factors.
- Control debt collection, expenses and stock levels.
- Decide when to pay bills.
- Compare original forecasts with actual to check that you are on target.
- Compare your profit and expenses with those from previous weeks, months, and years, to measure business growth (or decline.)
- Identify sales trends to maximise profit.
- Identify areas for improvement to achieve your profit goals.
- Choose which products to promote and which to drop.
- Avert financial disaster.

Analysing Your Performance

Below are examples of some of the statistics and records you could keep to help you to make important business decisions.

How to Check if Your Business is Growing

Gross Profit Margin

Gross Profit Margin percentage on sales =
(Total revenue – Cost of Goods Sold) ÷ Total Revenue x100

The gross profit margin is the difference between your revenue and costs. It can be used to measure the efficiency of your overall sales, individual products, or ranges. To find the gross profit margin of individual products, you should use the total revenue of each product (the selling price x units sold) and the total unit costs of the product sold.

To find out if your efficiency is improving you'll need to record the gross profit margin over time, and then make comparisons between the months or years.

Net Profit Margin

The net profit margin is another measurement of efficiency, which reveals how well your business converts revenue into real profit after all of your expenses.

Net Profit Margin =
   (Total Revenue – Expenses) ÷ Total Revenue   x100

The net profit margin will tell you the amount of profit you make for every £1 of sales revenue. A percentage of 58%, for example, means that for every £1 of sales you make, 58p is profit. Having a low net profit margin would indicate that your pricing strategies and expenses need to be reviewed. Having a very low net profit could spell disaster if you suffer a decline in sales. To spot such problems in advance, you'll need to record the net profit margin over time, and then make comparisons across the months or years.

How to Control your Expenses

An expenses breakdown will enable you to monitor your individual monthly outgoings. If you keep double-entry books this information can be easily copied and pasted into a spreadsheet and used to help you to pinpoint problems.

Figure 9.3 Example: Expenses Breakdown

	Rent	Phone	Advertising	Travel	Fees	Total
January	£500	£25	£130	£40	£28	£723
February	£500	£29	£150	£56	£44	£779

Multi-Sales Channel Expenses

You could monitor the expenses of each of your sales channels to see which channels are costing you the most to operate:

Figure 9.4 Example: Sales Channels Expenses

	Shop	Website	Home Parties	Auction Sites
January	£300	£100	£40	£56
February	£476	£89	£37	£79

However, just because one of your sales channels has high outgoings doesn't necessarily mean that it is draining your business and not efficiently generating profit. Therefore, a better method is to compare the net profit margins of each of your sales channels, as this will take into account the revenue from each, as well as its expenses, to give an indication of performance. You will need to apportion the costs that are not produced solely by one single channel, such as the depreciation of equipment that is shared by all sales channels.

How to Identify Sales Trends to Maximise Profit

Value and Number of Sales

Monitoring the number and value of the sales you make in a given time period, can help you spot patterns and trends. Many businesses analyse sales statistics month by month, but for more in-depth information, you could record it on a weekly, daily, or even hourly basis. Sales data can help to determine the best times to run Pay Per Click adverts and promotions, store opening times, how much stock and supplies to purchase, and the number of staff you'll need to meet expected demand at a given time.

In the 'Total Sales' columns, you can record the total number of sales, the total value of sales, bookings, website page hits, the number of people through your door, or any other factors that you think will provide useful information instead.

Once enough data has been gathered, you should be able to spot any patterns emerging.

Figure 9.5 Example: Sales Data Records

Hourly

	Total Sales
Hour 1	
Hour 2	
Hour 3	
Hour 4	
Hour 24	

Daily

	Total Sales
Day 1	
Day 2	
Day 3	
Day 4	
Day 31	

Weekly

	Total Sales
Week 1	
Week 2	
Week 3	
Week 4	
Week 52	

Monthly

	Total Sales
Month 1	
Month 2	
Month 3	
Month 4	
Month 12	

Individual Product Sales

A breakdown of the sales of each product can help you to decide how much stock you will need at various times of the year.

Figure 9.6 Monthly Sales Record

	Jan	Feb	Mar	Apr	May	Jun	Jul	Aug	Sep	Oct	Nov	Dec
Product A	11	12	6	1	0	0	0	1	9	18	20	23
Product B	18	22	20	21	21	19	20	21	21	22	23	24

In the example above, 'Product A' sells well during autumn and winter, but not in the summer months. Therefore, you would need to buy enough units by September and sell them all by the spring.

'Product B' seems to be a steady-selling product, and therefore, it will be relatively easy to maintain the appropriate stock levels throughout the year.

Sales and promotions, short-lived trends, and advertising campaigns can skew your sales data, so make a note of such events, and consider them when making repeat stock purchases.

Average Basket Value

It can help to know the average value of your sales:

> **Basket Value =**
> Total Sales (£) ÷ Number of Sales

If the average sale is £27, for instance, you should ask yourself what you could do to raise this to £30 or £35. Maybe you could offer free delivery or a gift when they spend over this amount, or try to cross-sell and up-sell more. The average value of each sale can be compared over time to check if it is increasing. If it is not, then you'll need to try a different approach to increase your customers' basket value.

How to Manage Your Stock

Stock Keeping Balance Sheet

A simple method to manage your stock is to keep a tally of all purchases of each product and then takeaway its sales and 'shrinkage' (defective or stolen) and restock any returns, as in the example below:

Figure 9.7 Stock Inventory Record

	Total Purchases	Total Sales	Total Shrinkage	Total Returns	Current Balance
Product A	150	89	0	7	68
Product B	60	10	1	0	49

If working with Microsoft Excel or similar, you can insert a link from a running total from the total individual product sales record (see page 142) to the total sales cell. It will then automatically update itself and provide you with up-to-date stock information.

Current Stock Value

Having too much money tied up in stock can cause cash flow problems, so it is beneficial to keep a record, as in Figure 9.8. Having a high value amount of stock of one product is not necessarily a problem if you are turning over the stock quickly.

Figure 9.8 Stock Value Record

	Unit Price	Stock Quantity	Total Value
Product A	£4.34	12	£52.08
Product B	£0.52	26	£13.52

The total value of your current stock is also a useful figure to have when selling the business, or taking out an insurance policy.

Contribution Margin of Product

Working out the profit contribution of each single SKU, product line, or brand, will tell you which products you should be focusing on, (because they are contributing the most profit), and which products you should investigate further or discontinue, (because they are performing poorly).

Figure 9.9 Product Contribution Margin

	Gross Profit £	Units Sold	£ Product Contribution	% Profit Contribution
Product A	£6.65	60	£399.00	53.99 %
Product B	£2.80	100	£280.00	37.89 %
Product C	£4.00	15	£60.00	8.12 %
	Total Gross Profit		**£739.00**	**≈ 100 %**

To work out the contribution margins of products you should make the following calculations:

1. Your Selling Price – Cost of Goods Sold = Gross Profit (£)
2. Gross Profit x Number of Units Sold = Product Contribution (£)
3. Product's Contribution (£) ÷ Total Gross Profit
4. x100 = Product Contribution (%)

Example:
Product A costs the retailer £4.34 and has a selling price of £10.99
1. £10.99 - £4.34 = £6.65
2. £6.65 x 60 = £399.00
3. £399.00 ÷ £739.00 = 0.5399
4. 0.5399 x 100 = 53.99%

Presenting the Data

In order to analyse the information properly, it needs to be presented in a user-friendly format. Some bookkeeping programs, such as Sage, automatically produce reports and charts to help you analyse data. Spreadsheet software such as Microsoft Excel can do the job just as well, although some of the formulas may take a bit of work if you are unfamiliar with it.

Making Improvements & Troubleshooting

Management accounting is, all too often, performed by small businesses when things aren't going well. Smart business owners continuously check performance indicators to give themselves advance warning of any problems before they become irreversible.

All businesses encounter financial aches and pains from time to time, such as failing to meet profit targets, or struggling to pay creditors on time. Such symptoms are caused by one or more of the three main problem areas; low incomings; high expenses; and poor cash flow management. If ignored, they can have a detrimental effect on your financial health. Fortunately, as you will see below, there are plenty of possible remedies for each.

Your Incomings are Too Low

A low gross profit, or even just feeling disappointed that your sales weren't as good as expected, are usually signs that you need to look at improving your incomings. Typically, it can take a few years before a new business starts generating the sort of profit that makes all the hard work worthwhile, so don't be overly concerned if you have just started up.

Remedies include:
- Negotiate a lower unit price from your supplier, take advantage of discounts, or find a different supplier or an alternative product.
- Modify your selling prices to achieve optimum revenue.
- Sell more by cross-selling, and increase basket value by up-selling.
- Discontinue poor performing products that have low profit margins and low sales volumes.
- Focus on the sales channels that bring in the most income.
- Increase your customer base with advertising and promotions.
- Make your products more attractive with free delivery, free gifts, etc.
- Diversify into new markets with new products or target markets.
- Identify and focus on your most profitable customers.

Your Expenses are Too High

Having out-of-control expenses is a common problem, which is easy to spot if there is a considerable difference between your incomings and the profit you are left with after you've calculated your outgoings.

Remedies include:
- Perform an expenses review (see below).
- Negotiate cheaper prices with landlords and suppliers.
- Lease rather than buy, or consider buying second hand.
- Find cheaper substitutes (e.g., would a flyer work instead of a

booklet?)
- Calculate the ROI (see below) for the sales channels with the highest outgoings.
- Reduce wastage and utilities.
- Reduce energy usage and upgrade to more efficient equipment.
- Focus less on poorer performing customers that drain your resources.
- Join forces with another business to share advertising, event stands, premises, etc.

Expenses Review

List all of your expenses in order from the biggest to smallest. For each expense starting with the biggest, you should ask yourself the following questions:

- Is it essential to my operation?
- Is it providing a high enough ROI (see below)?
- Are there any cheaper alternatives available?
- What will be the consequence of eliminating this expense in the short and long term? (Will it affect quality, brand image, or customer awareness?)

Sometimes the solution can be as simple as identifying the non-essential purchases and reducing or postponing them until your business has grown some more. In other cases, it may not be cost-effective to lower an expense. For example, you may be able to reduce your rent and rates, but it would mean you would have to relocate or downsize, which would increase short-term outgoings.

Return On Investment

Spending a large amount of money on a purchase isn't necessarily a bad thing as long as you get a good return on your investment (ROI.) To measure whether an expense such as advertising is generating a good ROI you should calculate the following:

ROI =
  (Gain from Investment – Cost of Investment) - Cost of Investment

ROI as a percentage =
                    x100

The calculation will help you decide if an expense will generate a high enough income to help you reach your profit targets. The higher the percentage the better.

You Have Cash Flow Problems

If you don't have enough money to pay bills on time then your business has cash flow problems. This could increase your expenses if your suppliers start charging you statutory interest, or you may incur bank fees if you need to take out a loan or overdraft to cover it.

Remedies include:

- Reduce the amount of money you have tied up in stock by consulting past sales data before making purchases.
- Increase stock turnover by increasing customers, advertising, and sales to release cash from stock.
- Make sure your debtors pay you on time by making your payment terms clear in your conditions. If they fail to pay on time, take action.

- Reduce the period of credit you give your customers.
- Take full advantage of credit terms that suppliers offer you; if you don't have to pay straightaway, then don't.
- Sell off surplus assets to release the cash.
- Increase your overdraft or take out a loan.
- Increase your prices.
- Find an investor or invest money of your own.

Note that none of the remedies suggests slashing prices, which is often the first thing that business owners consider doing when they encounter financial problems. This is a hasty reaction, but it should always be a last resort unless you are specifically trying to capture market share or are involved in a price war.

In the final chapter, we will look at how to plan for the future, and realise your vision for your pet accessories business.

Thinking about the Future

I n the early days, it can be hard to think ahead to the future when you are putting in very long hours each day and juggling many roles. Eventually though, as your business starts to become more established, you can slowly step back and reap the rewards; not just the financial benefits, but the flexibility and increased leisure time that owning a mature and stable enterprise brings.

Once you have survived the critical early years, your responsibilities as an owner will evolve. You should set challenging yet achievable objectives to drive your company forward, and plan long-term strategies to make your dream of running a *successful* pet accessories business a reality.

Increasing your revenue and your market share are probably the two most common future aims. How you achieve these though will depend on your businesses' situation. One thing is sure; you will need the support of your most important asset: your employees.

By understanding the strengths and weaknesses of your company, as well as the opportunities and threats that exist, you will be able to steer your business in the right direction.

SWOT Analysis

You'll need to decide the best way to grow and improve your business in the long-term. To do this, it usually helps to analyse your strengths, weaknesses, opportunities, and threats (SWOT).

Strengths / Weaknesses

Strengths are internal factors that you do well. They include assets, resources, specialities, and other factors that provide a competitive advantage. Weaknesses are internal aspects of your business that need to be improved because either your competitors perform them better or because they hinder your ability to meet targets.

- Brand and reputation
- Marketing strategy
- Experienced, skilled staff
- Customer service
- Level of competition
- Location
- Relationships with suppliers
- Equipment and technology
- Pricing
- Customer base
- Market share
- Online presence
- Unique products
- Financial position
- Stock management

Opportunities / Threats

Opportunities are external factors that could improve your business and enable you to meet targets. Threats are external factors that are out of your control, but could potentially harm your business. Some of the factors listed on p152 may not appear to be both an opportunity and a threat, but consider the consequences of not being able to take an opportunity (due to a lack of resources, for example.) If a competitor was to get a grant, or your customers adopted new technology, and your business did not, it could threaten your position in the market.

- Grants
- New technology
- Diversification
- Online presence
- Financial position
- Joint ventures
- Acquisitions
- Social changes

- Competitor's activities
- Competitor's pricing
- Exchange rate changes
- Interest rate changes
- Taxation changes
- Exporting to new markets
- Market growth/ decline
- Legal changes

The SWOT Analysis Matrix

To make it easier to see the bigger picture, you should insert the factors that affect your business into the appropriate boxes of a SWOT analysis, see Figure 10.1.

Figure 10.1 Example of a Completed SWOT Analysis

STRENGTHS	WEAKNESSES
• Relationships with suppliers • Equipment and technology • Stock management • Location	• Experienced, skilled staff • Customer service • Brand and reputation
OPPORTUNITIES	**THREATS**
• Grants • Online presence • New technology • Taxation changes	• Competitor's activities • Interest rate changes

Once you have completed a SWOT analysis matrix, you should have a better idea of your capabilities and limitations, and the possibilities for future growth and improvement. This will enable you to develop a long-term plan.

The Strategic Plan

The term 'strategic planning' might sound as though it belongs inside a corporate boardroom, but it is just another way of describing the process of developing the plans and goals that will help turn that vision into a reality.

To help you to formulate your strategic plan you should ask yourself the following three questions:

1. Where are we now? What is your monthly and annual turnover and profit? What percentage of market share do you possess? How satisfied are your customers? What is the public perception of your brand and level of awareness of your business? How competitive are you? Are you achieving your current goals and objectives with ease or difficulty? What are your strengths and weaknesses?

2. Where do we want to be? Where do you see your business in three, five, and ten year's time? What are your long-term goals? What is the business vision and mission? What is the best way to expand and improve? What opportunities exist?

3. How are you going to get there? What resources and skills do you need? What do the individual functions, such as marketing, need to do to help achieve the overall objectives? What operational processes need to be improved? What attitudes need to change? Where do you need to focus your efforts in the future?

Dream Big

People are often reluctant to aim high for fear of disappointment. Even if you don't turn every aspect of your vision into a reality, you will still be running a wonderfully successful and fulfilling business in a highly rewarding industry. Often, it is a good idea to ask yourself a fourth question when developing your strategic plan; where will we end up if we continue in the same direction? The answer to this is usually enough to motivate bigger ideas, after all, businesses have to grow just to maintain their current position.

You will still need to take into consideration the practicalities of future growth and improvement. Your vision could entail targeting new markets and increasing your customer base for example, which could require bigger premises and more resources. How you will obtain and finance these extra resources should be included in your plan. You should view the practicalities that are involved as challenges that you can overcome with good planning, rather than obstacles that will hamper your big ideas.

Setting Smart Objectives

By setting targets, you can regularly assess your performance and measure how much closer you are to your dream. You'll improve your success rate if the targets are 'SMART':

- **Specific** – targets need to describe exactly what you want to achieve, e.g., 'to increase market share', 'launch an online store', 'increase turnover', 'raise brand awareness'.
- **Measurable** – measurements such as '£10,000', '12%', and '50', will provide a means to measure your performance.
- **Attainable** – targets should be challenging yet attainable and you should know exactly what you need to do to achieve them.
- **Relevant** – your goals should support the mission and overall

vision of your business, and should be worthwhile.

- **Timely** – setting a completion date such as 'by 2025', 'in eight months,' or 'by July 19th' will improve your success rate.

An example of a smart target could be 'To increase sales turnover by 26% within 4 years.'

Evaluating Your Performance

Reviewing your strategic plan and evaluating your performance regularly will keep you focused on driving the business forward. If, for example, you aim to increase sales within twelve months then you should review your performance at six months or each quarter. You may need to modify your strategic plan whenever you achieve or set new objectives, or as new opportunities and threats arise. The strategic plan is not set in stone; it is a means of steering a business to its potential.

Transforming Your Role

When owners first launch a business, they often end up doing everything; accounting, marketing, customer service, IT, picking orders, etc. Sixteen-hour days are not uncommon. Once the business is stable though, you can start to focus more on the future and less on the menial day-to-day tasks. With fewer responsibilities, you could reduce your working hours, and as much as you may love being the boss, who wouldn't say no to a little bit more leisure time?

In 'The Four-Hour Workweek', author Timothy Ferriss explains how outsourcing is one way to achieve freedom from the tasks that you dislike and free up your time. He recommends outsourcing to other companies that provide 'remote assistants' who specialise in performing tasks such as answering emails and telephone calls, fulfilling orders, bookkeeping, social networking, search engine optimisation, etc.

Outsourcing aspects of a service-based business, which requires your physical presence, can be trickier. Delegating tasks to staff will reduce the time you spend working on menial chores and create more family time, while utilising wireless technology such as smart-phones, tablets, and laptops will enable you to run your business anywhere, at anytime.

A Final Thought

All the talk in the media of economic downturns can be worrying to owners and off-putting to those considering starting up their own business. However, not all markets go into recession, and the designer pet accessories market could be one of them. After all, the last things people will stop spending on are their children and pets.

In a downturn, consumer-purchasing habits are likely to change though, so small businesses still need to be flexible and forward thinking if they are to survive and prosper.

References

Baines, P., Fill, C., and Page, K. 2010. *Marketing, Second Edition.* Oxford: OUP.

Ferriss, T. 2009. The Four-Hour Workweek: Escape 9-5, Live Anywhere, and Join The New Rich. New York: Crown.

Godin, S. 1999. Permission Marketing: Turning Strangers into Friends and Friends into Customers. New York: Simon & Schuster.

Middleston, S. 2010. Build a Brand in 30 Days: With Simon Middleton, The Brand Strategy Guru. Chichester: Capstone.

Nagle, T., Hogan, J. and Zale, J. 2010. *The Strategy and Tactics of Pricing, 5th Edition*. Prentice Hall.

Weetman, P. 2010. *Management Accounting, Second Edition.* Financial Times/ Prentice Hall.

Websites
www.businesslink.gov.uk
www.cipd.co.uk
www.designcouncil.org.uk
www.elmsbury.com
www.inc.com

Resources

Pet suppliers and B2B Directories
www.alibaba.com
www.aliexpress.com
www.batleys.co.uk
www.busytrade.com
www.globalsources.com
www.makro.co.uk
www.princeprincesspetwear.co.uk
www.smallvolume.com
www.thewholesaler.co.uk

Pet Shows and Trade Events
www.crufts.org.uk
www.globalpetexpo.org
www.interzoo.com
www.londonpetshow.co.uk
www.lovepetsshow.co.uk
www.patsshow.co.uk

Pet Trade Publications
www.petbusinessworld.co.uk
www.petgazette.biz
www.petproductmarketing.co.uk
www.pettradeworld.com

General Business Information
www.britishchambers.org.uk
www.companieshouse.gov.uk
www.gov.uk/browse/business
www.hmrc.gov.uk

Marketing and Networking
https://twitter.com
www.bttradespace.com
www.constantcontact.com
www.facebook.com
www.google.co.uk/adwords
www.mailchimp.com
www.surveymonkey.com
www.linkedin.com

Ecommerce, Website, and Mobile Site Providers
www.ekmpowershop.com
www.jimdo.com
www.lemonstand.com
www.magentocommerce.com
www.mymcart.com
www.oscommerce.com
www.prestashop.com
www.shopify.com
www.vendorshopsocial.com
www.weebly.com
www.wordpress.org
www.wordpress.com
www.zen-cart.com

Index

Z